Hats
Fiona Clark

The Costume Accessories Series
General Editor: Dr Aileen Ribeiro

B. T. BATSFORD LTD
LONDON

Acknowledgment

ISBN 0 7134 3774 X

Typeset by Tek-Art Ltd, Kent
and printed in Great Britain by
Anchor Brendon Ltd,
Tiptree, Essex
B. T. Batsford Ltd
4 Fitzhardinge Street
London W1H 0AH

The author would like to thank the staff of all the
museums listed at the end of this book for their
kindness in making their collections available and
preparing material for photography. Special thanks
are due to Miss Jane Paternoster, who typed the
manuscript, and to Mr Graham Pink who helped
with photography and many other things besides.

Contents

List of Illustrations

Brown (*Birmingham City Art Gallery*).

33 *Punch* cartoon 'On the Boulogne Pier', 1866 (*Worthing Library*).

34 Photograph showing man in hat c.1880s (*Worthing Museum*).

35 Dubosch & Gillingham advertisement for hair pieces, *The Lady*, 1905 (*Worthing Museum*).

36 Photograph of three ladies in hats, c.1905-6 (*Worthing Museum*).

37 Photo o' lady in tweed cap, c.1906 (*Worthing Museum*).

38 Photograph showing Heather Firbank in rose trimmed hat, c.1910 (*Victoria & Albert Museum*).

39 Toque trimmed with cock pheasant 1908-10 (*Museum of Costume & Textiles, Nottingham*).

40 Chenille hat with owl's head and wing, c.1912 (*Royal Albert Memorial Museum, Exeter*).

41 Claret straw hat by Lambert Bernheim, 1914 (*The Museum of London*).

42 Advertisement for hats by H. C. Russell, *The Tatler*, 1914 (*Worthing Museum*).

43 Printed suede hat, c.1924 (*Platt Hall*).

44 Black felt hat by Agnès, 1929-30 (*Museum of Costume, Bath*).

45 Pink felt hat by Maison Ross, c.1925 (*Museum of Costume, Bath*).

46 Barker's advertisement for hats, early 1930s (*Worthing Museum*).

47 Advertisement for hats, winter 1939 (*Worthing Museum*).

48 Group of three hats worn by Margot Fonteyn, mid-1940s-1950s (*Museum of Costume, Bath*).

49 Group of four hats worn by Mrs Hill, late 1940s-1950s (*Museum of Costume & Textiles, Nottingham*).

50 Hat by David Shilling (*courtesy of David Shilling & Revlon*).

51 'Bank Holiday', by William Strang, 1912 (*The Tate Gallery, London*).

52 Photograph showing crowd in front of Luton Town Hall, summer 1911 (*The Luton Museum & Art Gallery*).

53 Portrait of the Prince of Wales by John St Helier Lander, c.1922 (*Leeds Art Galleries*).

54 Advertisement for hats by Simpsons of Piccadilly, 1938.

55 Homburg hat, 1930s, (*Worthing Museum*).

56 Photograph of woman making boater hats, 1936.

57 Two embroidered night caps, early 17th century (*Museum of Costume & Textiles, Nottingham*).

58 'Lord George Graham in his Cabin', c.1745, by William Hogarth.

59 'Femme de Qualite' engraving after J. D. de St Jean, 1693 (*Victoria & Albert Museum*).

60 'L'atelier De Lingerea', c.1805 (*City of Manchester Art Galleries*).

61 Morning cap, 1825-8 (*Worthing Museum*).

62 Dress cap in black lace and velvet ribbon, c.1865 (*Worthing Museum*).

63 Advertisement showing boudoir caps, 1917 (*Worthing Museum*).

64 Group of boudoir caps, 1920s (*Worthing Museum*).

65 Miniature milliner's model bonnets, 1850s-1860s (*Platt Hall*).

66 Advertisement for hats by Madame Tucker Widgery, 1890s (*Worthing Museum*).

67 'The Hat Shop', by Henry Tonks, c.1905 (*Birmingham City Art Gallery*).

68 Bill sent to the Ranee of Pudakota from Caroline Reboux (*Museum of Costume, Bath*).

69 Letter sent to Ranee of Pudakota from Reboux (*Museum of Costume, Bath*).

70 'The Mad Hatter', illustration by John Tenniel to *Alice's Adventures in Wonderland*, 1865.

71 Hat stretchers, brushes and guards, 19th & 20th centuries (*Worthing Museum*).

72 *Punch* cartoon, 'Brushing Pa's new hat', c.1860s

Introduction

This book was planned as one of a series of four covering the major accessories to dress. Each one aims to provide a general background to the subject, beginning at the starting point of 1600 which is common to the whole series. A specific bias has been given towards actual specimens in museum collections and the majority of photographs have been drawn from this source. A brief description of the principal collections of hats in England has been given at the end of this book, and it is hoped that this will encourage students and enthusiasts to discover this material for themselves.

There are some points to bear in mind when setting out to look at hats in museums. Firstly, hats cannot be expected to survive in quantity when dating prior to the eighteenth century — earlier examples are rare and limited to the major collections. Secondly, all social classes re-fashioned clothing in the eighteenth and nineteenth centuries in an attempt to get the maximum mileage from quality materials. Women's hats, which changed style from season to season, were particularly tempting to re-trim and re-shape and many museum specimens are either denuded of their trimmings or are an unhappy hybrid of different styles and dates. They should, therefore, be considered in the light of other evidence, visual and literary, and allowances made. However, when good-quality hats have miraculously survived in something close to their original condition they testify better than any fashion plate or even photograph to the exquisite delicacy, wealth of detail and skilled co-ordination of different materials which is the special province of the art of millinery. Men's hats are more likely to have suffered from simple hard wear but again good specimens provide telling evidence for the hatter's traditional skills and regard for quality.

Men's and women's hats have been treated separately in the historical narrative, since, although the main social and stylistic changes affect both, the pace of change in men's headgear has been so much slower. The main sequence of chapters cover headgear, notably hats and bonnets, but also caps worn for sport and country wear. Caps worn indoors are given a separate chapter towards the end of the book. This is done for convenience of description, although it is a fact that the distinctions between indoor and outdoor headgear, as with most of the social distinctions relating to the wearing of hats, did not become hard and fast until the nineteenth century. The fashions described are principally those which obtained in England, but relate also the the United States of America.

The surface movements of the subject are so bewildering that it may be helpful at the start to outline some of the constant factors, even at the risk of over-simplification. Hats became an important accessory for men earlier than for women, being highly fashionable from the fifteenth century. The same tendency which has been noticed in operation in other aspects of men's clothes also applies here, namely that new styles are introduced at an informal level, for sports, and evolve into formal fashionable wear. This process takes a long time: the bowler worn on mid-Victorian beaches took nearly a hundred years to become part of the caricature of an ultra conventional city businessman. It is important to note that men's hats have tended to make a symbolic statement, rather than a purely visual one. The most durable symbols have been the tall stiff hat, representing bourgeois authority, which comes to the fore in the nineteenth century and the soft felt hat, symbolic of democracy and revolution, which similarly emerged triumphant between the two world wars.

Hats did not become an important part of high fashion for women until the end of the eighteenth century, but made up for their slow start by an astonishing rate of change during the last two centuries. The female hat, which is less limited than any other item of clothing by the need to fit the body (it can merely sit, perch, or even appear to float), is therefore a sensitive barometer of visual change. Millinery has thrived best during artistic movements which have a strong element of fantasy or retrospection: Romanticism, Aestheticism and

Surrealism have spurred its greatest achievements. The whole span of two hundred years between roughly 1750 and 1950, which can be described as the great age of millinery, can also be seen as the rise and fall of the conception of romantic femininity. Perhaps because mediaeval women first adopted hats in the current masculine style for those active pursuits such as riding and travelling, for which their own veils and hoods were too restricting, the hat remained a symbol of emancipation during the eighteenth and nineteenth centuries. The bonnet, whose enclosing form resembled the hood and veil, gradually took over the role of the modest and conventional choice in headgear, ending in the Edwardian period as part of the uniform of mature age.

For the last twenty years or so, hats have ceased to be part of the everyday clothing of men and women. It is the author's experience in talking to clubs and groups that this break in the story has not diminished interest in the history of hats — indeed the frustrated desire to wear decorative headgear may even have heightened the interest. Yet in face of this general neglect of hats most people today still choose to mark the important occasions of their lives by wearing one — this surely is evidence of how deeply rooted is the urge to dignify and decorate our heads with a hat.

1

Men's Hats 1600-1800

The essential characteristics of men's hats during the four centuries dealt with in this study appear together for the first time during the late fourteenth and early fifteenth centuries. The form of hats at this time comprised a distinct brim and crown, the latter in a variety of shapes all emphasizing height; the chief materials, fur felt and straw plaited in strips, both new at this period, were to remain the staples of hat manufacture; their trimmings of feathers and hatbands, also innovations, would be consistently used over three centuries. Moreover, men's hats at this time were not only newly fashionable, but were already used to express superiority of social status, especially within the developing Guild system. [1]

In the earlier Middle Ages, among a variety of hoods and caps mostly worn by poorer people, a style of hat appeared in the twelfth century which spanned all levels of society. This had a low crown and broad brim and was a revival of the Greek 'petasos', which was worn by travellers, pilgrims and students. This style would become fashionable again, as we shall see.

Men's hats have a more limited vocabulary of form and decoration than women's, but in two respects they are more expressive. The first is that simply because of the tendency of masculine hats to conformity, very subtle variations are possible in the individual's manner of wearing them. These nuances are inevitably more difficult for the modern eye to detect than the overtly decorative changes in women's headgear, though occasionally a clue can be found in the ephemeral literature of the time. Secondly, because the hat clothes the seat of intellect, and since this attribute has largely been more highly valued in men than in women, men's hats in particular express social and political aspirations.

The two main types of hat have a corresponding symbolism. The tall hat, generally stiff, stands for a gamut of ideas ranging from formal elegance, through active endeavour in trades, professions and moral rectitude, to Protestantism and the bourgeoisie, which are the religion and class most associated with

these ideals. By contrast, the low-crowned, broad-brimmed hat, generally of flexible material, is associated with informality, country life, intellectuals and artists and even with egalitarianism and revolution. The permutations of these two groups of symbols are very wide and the whole range cannot be inferred in every reappearance of the style. Yet they provide a recurrent and unifying theme in the development of men's headgear.

At the opening of the seventeenth century the currently fashionable form of hat was the 'copotain' with a tall, slightly tapered crown and a moderate brim. This style had reached England in the middle of the previous century, probably from Spain, and accorded with the formal elegance which was the hallmark of Spanish fashion. During the reign of James I these hats were made of a variety of materials including beaver, wool felt, shag (a kind of hatter's plush) and silk and velvet stiffened with buckram or card. Although bright colours such as scarlet were used, the most popular colour was black, a tendency noticeable long before the nineteenth century. Jacobean gallants usually wore their hats tilted, to the side or back, and decorated with jewelled brooches or hatbands.

Approximately at the time of the accession of Charles I a new style of hat came into vogue with a lower crown and wider brim, invariably made in a flexible felt. This last feature made it adaptable and a large number of variations in the manner of wearing it can be seen in contemporary paintings: the brim could be 'cocked' (turned up) to right or left, turned up entirely in the front like a halo, [2] obscuring the crown, or 'coggled' throughout and forming a wavy line. [3] In James Stutely's play *The Lady of Pleasure* written in 1735, a would-be gallant has just bought a fashionable outfit and is being instructed on how to wear it. 'You wear your hat too like a citizen. . . place it with best advantage of your hair. Is your feather moulted? . . . it should spread over like a canopy.' This fashionable decoration of a trailing plume can be seen in Van Dyck's portrait of the king in the same year.[4] The period between 1620 and 1640 was a time when men's clothes gave an effect of military swagger and Baroque movement and these hats with their undulating brims and sweeping feathers made an important contribution to this look.

Hats had an especially important status in the wardrobe of a man of fashion throughout the first half of the seventeenth century. One reason for this was the preference for hats made of beaver felt, sometimes known by the Latin name for the animal as 'castors'. Felt made from beaver's fur was the quality material for men's hats from the fourteenth to the mid-nineteenth century and the process of felting the fur was always difficult and costly (see Chapter 11). However, supplies of beaver fur were running out in Europe by the seventeenth century and the situation improved only when skins were imported from the New World after 1670. Where Philip Stubbes had

2 *Silk cocked hat, wig and wig bag, all belonging* ▷ *to Thomas Worsley, mid-18th century. Worsley lived at Platt Hall, Manchester, which now houses The Gallery of English Costume.*

quoted 40 shillings as an outrageous price for a beaver hat in 1583,[5] Samuel Pepys noted in his diary for 1661 that a beaver hat had cost him 45 shillings. These hats were accordingly greatly treasured and Pepys records that on an evening ride in April 1662 he 'was in nothing troubled but by the badness of my hat, which I borrowed to save my beaver'. He was similarly upset the previous year when his hat fell off his head into the water 'by which it was spoiled and I ashamed of it'.

From around 1640 to 1660 a stiff hat with a tall, tapering crown was popular, a revival of the earlier copotain, and was known as a 'sugarloaf'. A fashionable trimming for this hat was a bunch of looped ribbons similar to that currently worn on breeches and shoes. This type of hat used to be popularly associated with the Puritans but any particular distinction of dress among Puritans other than a tendency to restraint in trimmings has been denied by recent

1 *Black felt hat, c.1650. Only the size suggests that this example is a man's rather than a woman's hat of the mid-17th century. The 'sugarloaf' crown and the brim are very much stiffer than they would have been a decade earlier.*

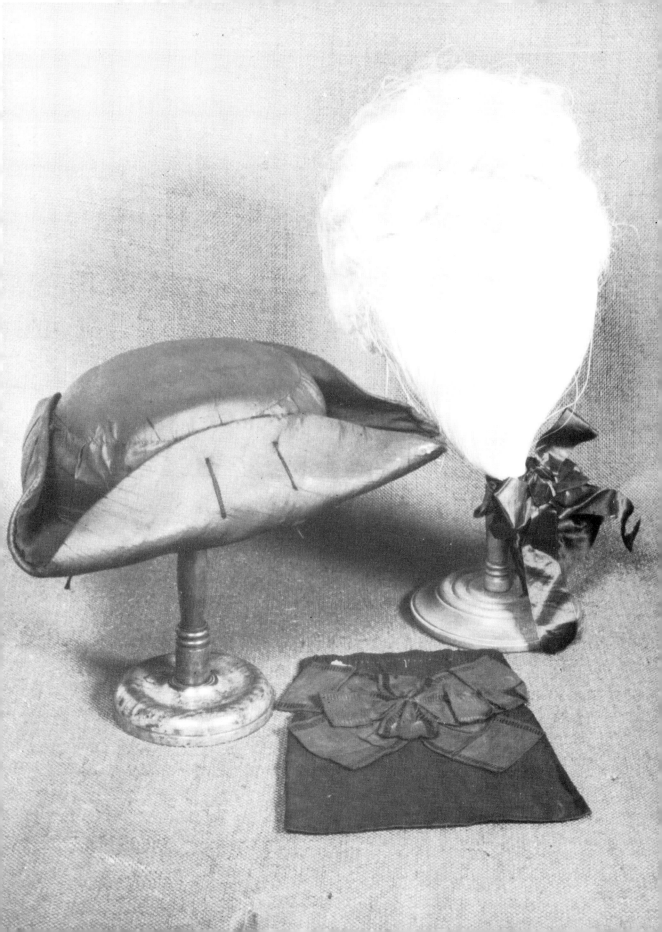

costume historians. However, this fashion does coincide with the Commonwealth and it is possible that its stiffness and severity was sympathetic to the mood of the times.

After 1660 the status and appearance of men's hats was to be radically altered by the adoption of wigs. Pepys had his long natural locks cut off to make a wig in 1663, the same year as Charles II himself. A much shallower crowned, broader brimmed hat came into use around 1670 and was sometimes known as the 'French hat', a name reflecting the influence of the court of Louis XIV which dominated fashions in the second half of the century. For the rest of the seventeenth century it seemed as if every attempt was being made to get the hat out of the way, a natural reaction to the great heat generated by the wearing of wigs. First the entire back brim was turned up in the 'Monmouth' cock and by 1690 a three-cornered cock had practically disposed of the brim altogether. A metal braid or 'lace' edge was added to the brims from 1675.

The hat thus produced, with its stiff, rounded crown and sides turned back to form a neat triangle, is familiar to us by its nineteenth-century name, the 'tricorne'. The style was so universally adopted throughout the greater part of the eighteenth century that for contemporaries it was sufficient to name only the variations and exceptions. The principal varieties were the more dashing styles worn by the military and the civilian dandies. Chief of these was the 'Kevenhuller' which featured a front pinched to project sharply forward — this can be clearly seen in Gainsborough's portrait of Mr and Mrs Robert Andrews in 1748. The 'Nivernois', popular in the 1760s, had very deep rolled-up brim and was also known as the 'waterproof' hat because of its umbrella-like protection. Small hats were fashionable in the 1730s, larger ones in the 1740s and 50s and exceptionally small hats were worn by the dandies or 'Macaronis' of the 1770s. The material used was

3 Richard Moreton with his nephew and niece by Arthur Devis, c.1760. The man's cocked hat has been casually propped against the chair — similar outdoor 'conversation piece' portraits depict hats carried under the arm or worn on the head. No inflexible rule governed hat wearing in this century.

generally wool felt, beaver felt or a mixture of beaver and rabbit fur known as a 'demi-castor'. The colour was almost invariably black – Beau Nash, Master of Ceremonies at Bath, would distinguish himself from the fashionable crowd by wearing a white beaver hat. The brims were edged with metal 'lace' or braid and a button and loop was always attached to the left cock. Cockades were worn with military styles, and fringes of feathers, a survival from the nodding plumes of the seventeenth century, were worn until 1760. For court wear, the button might be replaced with diamonds.

For the eighteenth-century gentleman the three-cornered hat had become a statutory requirement of dress which did not contribute greatly to its decorative effect. The latter was provided by the great variety of wig styles invented during the century and by the rich materials and decorations employed for dress suits. It was important to have a hat about one's person as a mark of good breeding, but whether it was worn or carried, indoors or out, did not matter, except in the presence of a social superior. Thus portrait groups show men on the same occasions either wearing or carrying hats. [6] In the 1760s this practice was acknowledged in the creation of the 'chapeau bras', a flat tricorne specifically for carrying under the arm.

4 Sir Brooke Boothby, by Joseph Wright of Derby, 1781. This shows a round felt hat worn with a frock coat, both representing the informal wear of the English gentleman which, within a few years, would be enthusiastically echoed in France. Sir Brooke proclaims himself a progressive intellectual by holding a copy of Rousseau's book.

An alternative to the three-cornered hat for those below the first rank of fashion was the round hat, essentially a felt hat without the turned-back brims. Artisans wore these in a soft, 'flapped' form (as they had in the seventeeth century) and a more rigid form was worn by the lower clergy and the learned professions. Paintings by George Stubbs in the 1760s frequently depict grooms wearing these hats. Lord Chesterfield noticed that it was fashionable among the smart set in the 1730s to adopt the dress of their social inferiors and wear 'slouched' hats and unpowdered hair. [7] During the next forty years, as the gentry and aristocracy began to spend more time in sporting pursuits and in improving their country estates, they came to view country life as the English gentleman's true milieu. During the 1760s they began to wear the sporting frock coat increasingly as an

5a *Bicorne hat, c.1796.*

---

everyday dress and a decade later the round hat was adopted as a riding hat in preference to the peaked jockey cap previously worn for the purpose. During the 1780s these hats were increasingly worn and were particularly sympathetic to artists and intellectuals –

5b *The inside of this hat shows the stamp which recorded payment of the hat tax. This tax was first imposed in 1783 but amended in 1796, substituting a stamp for a paper lable as proof of payment.*

Goethe had his portrait painted in one [8] and so did Sir Brooke Boothby, reading a copy of Rousseau's book (see fig. 4).

During the 1780s an even more stylized hat, later called the 'bicorne', was adopted for formal wear. This was cocked at the back and front only, forming a half circle. The three-cornered hat gradually declined in popularity while the round hat was more widely adopted. Its crown rose in the 1770s and again in the 1790s. In the late 1790s the brim grew smaller and the sides were rolled towards the crown. At the end of the century, on their natural, unpowdered heads, men were wearing a top hat in all but name.

2

Women's Hats 1600-1800

Women first wore hats at a comparatively late stage in the history of European dress and it was not until the eighteenth century that the first distinctive hat style for women appears. The two centuries dealt with in this chapter see hats for women move from the fringes to the very forefront of fashionable dress.

The teaching of the Church in the Middle Ages required a married women to conceal her hair in public, and veils and hoods were better adapted to this purpose than hats. During the fourteenth century women began to borrow the current masculine style of hat for active pursuits such as riding and travelling. By the reign of Elizabeth I, these borrowed styles were worn for a greater variety of informal occasions. Jacobean women wore the copotain hat in essentially the same style as the men's, but generally straight on the head rather than at an angle. Most of the varieties of hood worn during the previous reign, and in direct line of descent from mediaeval headgear, barely survived into the seventeenth century. When the copotain was succeeded in male fashion by the larger felt 'cavalier' style hat, women followed suit. Though fashionable women wore these hats for informal wear and active pursuits there is evidence that they were particularly espoused by middle-class women, for whom they were everyday wear. Thomas Platter noted in 1599 that 'English Burgher women usually wear high hats covered in velvet or silk for headgear'. [1]

This difference became more marked after around 1630 when fashion began to discover the allure of 'natural' or less confined hair. By this date the side hair was not included in the bun but was heavily crimped and frizzed; by 1645 the side locks fell loosely as corkscrew curls. This hairstyle led to an increasing reluctance on the part of upper-class women to cover their heads. This trend is illustrated in the engravings of Wenzel Hollar, a Boheman artist working in England in the 1640s. The lady of fashion who is depicted as 'Spring' in his *Four Seasons* series goes bareheaded in her elegant garden, while 'Summer' wears only a veil of light, transparent gauze to protect

her complexion. 'Winter' wears a hood of dark silk, loosely gathered into a band at the neck, which was a new style in 1640 and was to continue in fashion until the late eighteenth century. By contrast, the mayor's and merchant's wives in Hollar's *Ornatus Muliebris* series of the same date remain faithful to the current masculine style of felt hat with high crown and wide brim, worn over a linen cap.

Interest in naturalness in hair changed after the Restoration to a fascination with increased elaboration and artificiality in hairstyles. During the 1660s the side curls were wired out from the head while in 1670 a fringe of curls was mounted high on the forehead. This new trend only served to confirm the decline in hat wearing among the fashionable, save only with riding dress. By the 1690s it was necessary to support the mass of front curls with a wire frame or 'palisade' and the 'fontange' cap was the only head-dress which adorned this style. Even when the 'tour' hairstyle went out of fashion suddenly after 1710 to be followed by neat heads with top knots or close curls, fashionable taste ran to little round-eared caps rather than hats (see Chapter 9).

In the 1730s, at the same time as a few young dandies began to affect the slouched felt hats worn by their grooms, ladies began to be widely depicted in country house parks and town pleasure gardens wearing the flat-crowned straw hats which also appear on milkmaids and haymakers. The fashion for the rustic straw hat which seems to appear so suddenly actually had a very long gestation. By the seventeenth century a conventional 'shepherdess' or 'milkmaid' dress had been devised which was employed for pageants, masques and fashionable portraiture. This featured loose draperies and a wide-brimmed hat. The material is not discernible from portraits, but descriptions of masque dress specify straw hats as a 'rustic' attribute. [2] These may have been an actual feature of country dress in England at the time. Pepys says of a visit to Hatfield, Hertfordshire, in 1667, that the women of his party 'had pleasure in putting on some straw hats which are much worn in

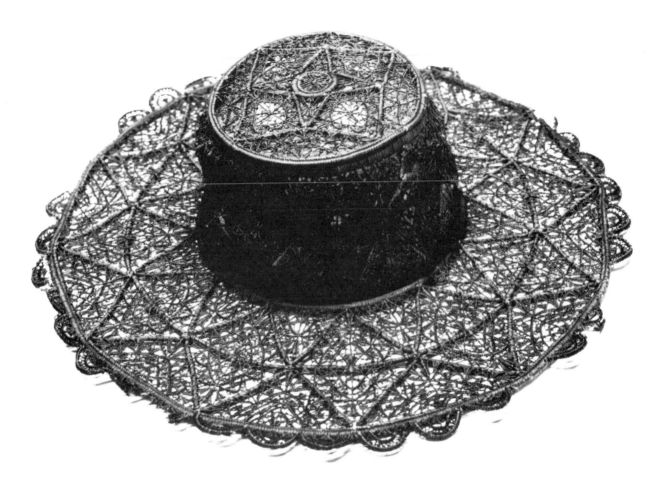

this country and did become them mightily, but especially my wife'.

The earliest records of the English straw-plaiting industry date from around this time. In 1681 Thomas Baskerville noted of Dunstable that 'some people of this town are here very curious in making straw hats'. Seven years later, a petition by the straw plaiters states that 14,000 people in Bedfordshire, Buckinghamshire and Hertfordshire lived by making straw hats. Since visual records of coutnry life are scanty before the fashionable adoption of the hat in the 1730s, it is difficult to judge how widely the custom of wearing straw hats had spread among country women in the seventeenth century. Other sources besides Pepys suggest that fashionable people were already attracted to the idea of wearing straw hats before 1730: the king and queen witnessed a similar scene to that at Hatfield in Hampton Court in 1719. [3] The only hats which survive from this period do not throw any light on their manner of wearing. Both come from great English country houses, one, tantalizingly, from Hatfield itself (see fig. 6). Yet their

6 Hat of fine cane, plaited in openwork patterns. Diameter of brim: 17½ in. This hat from the Foley estate, Hereford, is associated with Queen Anne. It is very similar in size and method of manufacture to one preserved at Hatfield House and said to have been worn by Queen Elizabeth I. The exact date of both examples is still a mystery, but is possibly late 17th century. The intricate patternwork suggests that they were imported from Italy for aristocratic use in England.

intricate construction suggests they were more likely to have been products of the older and more sophisticated straw-hat industry centred on Tuscany in Italy, which is recorded as being well established in the sixteenth century. [4]

The 'shepherdess' hat which emerged in the 1730s remained highly fashionable until the mid 1770s. Yet it remained an 'undress' fashion which would not have been tolerated with 'full dress'. [5] Usually worn over white caps with ribbon ties left hanging or used as a carrying handle, they were essentially garden hats made significant at a time when the country park was increasingly the preoccupation of the English gentleman and his wife, and pleasure gardens the focus of social life in the capital. The fashion was contemporary with the taste for 'conversation piece' portraiture, showing the sitters at ease in precisely this kind of setting. Foreigners who visited England in the eighteenth century noted both that these straw hats were essentially an English feature, and that they were common to all classes, with differences only of quality. [6]

'Conversation piece' portraits make it possible for us to note minor changes in the style. In the 1730s hats tended to be small and there was a brief fashion for pointed witches' crowns. During the 1740s they tended to have flexible, floppy brims, sometimes bound around the face, bonnet style. [7] in the 1750s the brim was often turned up sharply at front and back, [8] while in the early 1760s the hat stiffened and was worn at a very straight angle (see Plate 1). This straight line shows 'Chinoiserie' influence, also appearing in pointed crowns. Mushroom-shaped crowns were another variation early in this decade. [9] By the end of the decade the rising height of hairstyles imposed a forward tilt on hats.

Enough examples of this fashion survive in museum collections to give us in addition a detailed picture of the variety of materials and trimmings used. Chip or willow straw, imported from Holland, was frequently covered with silk taffeta, black being the most popular colour. [10] The usual trimming for these hats was loops of ribbon surrounding the crown, which echo the 'plastic ornaments' of wadded silk used on dresses and indicate a date in the 1750s or 60s. Very finely woven straw, made from an improved wheat developed by the Tuscan industry in this century and known as leghorn, is recorded as being widely used but examples have not survived. English straw does not appear to have been widely used until the end of the century. Vellum and horsehair were other choices and paper was used in a variety of ways, embossed to imitate straw; [11] cut in fine strips and woven as straw; [12] or as fine cut-out ornaments placed beneath fine net. [13] Both horsehair and paper hats were advertised in the *Salisbury Journal* for 1756, horsehair at 9 shillings a dozen, paper from 1 shilling 5 pence to 3 shillings a dozen.

By the late 1760s two new professions had emerged in France which were to have a profound influence on the development of female hats. Alphonse Legros, who founded an Academy of Hair in the 1760s and wrote a treatise on the subject, and Leonard, hair-dresser to Marie Antoinette, were the first practitioners of their craft to become celebrities in society. Their creations, from the tall, decorated toupée of the 1770s to the frizzed hedgehog styles of the 1780s, have been described as late examples of the Rococo style applied to dress. [14] In a similar vein was the work of the milliner who emerged in the 1760s as an arbiter of fashion, rather than purely a supplier of materials (see Chapter 10). The milliner decorated the dresses which were manufactured by the tailor with lace, gimp and artificial flowers and made caps and hats to complete the outfit. Through these new professions an element of frivolity, fantasy and decoration was added to women's fashion, which was precisely the climate in which hats were to thrive during the nineteenth century.

What happened when the English rustic straw hat was taken up and given French 'chic' can be seen in the great acceleration of change in hat styles during the 1770s, 80s and 90s. This was partly promoted by the first magazines of fashion, which appeared during this time. During the 1780s, hats began to be worn not only for 'undress' wear, but also with 'half dress' and 'full dress' — degrees of formal wear. Full dress hats tended to be smaller than undress styles, but more profusely decorated. Profusion of trimmings was also a new feature, and included the first use of artificial flowers on hats. In this decade artists depicted women wearing hats in all situations, including sitting at home and sewing; [15] but accurate or not, these pictures reflect how indispensable hats had become to the fashionable image. Other aspects of dress changed less rapidly during this time, as if all vitality was concentrated in the extraordinary flowering of headgear. Hats had become, and were to remain until recent times, the major costume accessory.

The high toupée of the 1770s posed a problem for hat design. At first the flat shepherdess style was worn with an extreme forward tilt or else very small hats were worn on the front of the head. At the end of the decade, two completely new shapes were invented, both with deep crowns which fitted over the coiffure. One was beehive shaped, the other had a soft, puffed crown and down-turning brims, usually made of silk over a framework. The latter was called variously the 'balloon', 'parachute' or 'lunardi' all names commemorating the pioneer balloon ascent of 1783. This style, always in black silk, became a popular rural style which survived until the end of the century. [16]

By 1783 the coiffure was dressed wide rather than high, an effect achieved by frizzing and crimping

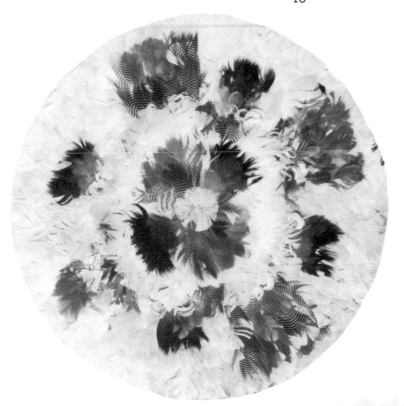

7 Hat covered with guinea fowl and cock's feathers, on a base of stiffened cotton, lined pink silk. Diameter: 14 in. This hat, together with the one illustrated in fig. 8, comes from a group of 12 hats of mid-18th century date which had been preserved at Culver House, near Exeter.

8 Hat made of stiffened silk ribbon, gathered and stitched together as a spiral, forming a point at the apex. This point has become crushed, but in its original condition the hat would have appeared to be in the Chinese taste. Diameter: 18 in, c.1760. From the Culver House collection (see fig. 7).

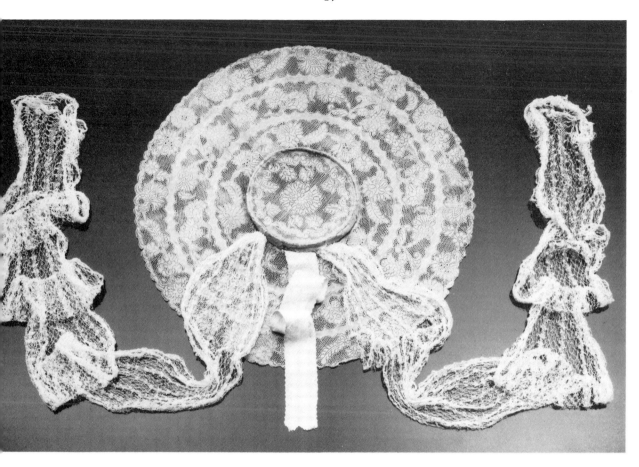

9 Hat made of vellum covered on both sides with beige silk, the three layers stamped through with an openwork 'lace' pattern. Single streamer of cream silk ribbon and long ties of white netted cotton. Diameter: 17 in, 1750-70.

rather than by wire supports. A variety of very wide brimmed styles were worn, with a pronounced sideways tilt or with the brims dipping down at front and back. 'Boater' style hats were worn with shallow crowns and rigid brims and the balloon style hats continued to be worn. Both these styles often had a falling frill of lace attached to the brim. During the later part of the decade height was introduced, and tall crowned hats were described as having 'the brim

10 Black felt hat with streamers of multicoloured ▷ silk ribbon, 1790-1800. This would have been worn with a riding habit, which at this date was fashionable as a promenade dress as well as on horseback.

made very narrow and falling down like the roof of a house' (1787).[17] Large veils were attached to the back of these.

From 1792 the fashionable exuberance in hair-styles had passed and hair was dressed close to the head, shorn or in loose knots on the crown. As we might perhaps expect from a post-revolutionary period, styles were chaotic and distinctions between 'undress' and 'full dress' were blurred. Tall crowned 'top hat' styles were worn (see fig. 10) and small helmet-shaped hats were popular. Most significant were two new bonnet forms; one a small chip hat bound to the head and tied under the chin, and

the other the 'poking' hat, introduced at the end of the decade, with 'a long projection like the beak of a snipe'.[18] Face veils were also introduced.

By the close of the eighteenth century all the distinguishing features of millinery which would be popular during the next two centuries were already established: great seasonal change and variety; frivolity and wit in the use of trimmings, especially artificial flowers and veils, even the bonnet form itself. The hat was seen by contemporaries as the major costume accessory and an essential attribute of the new ideal of romantic femininity which had emerged.

3

Women's Hats 1800-1850

During the first fifteen years of the nineteenth century women were exploring the variety of headgear which they had discovered in the closing years of the last century. The current hairstyle, a loose knot of curls at the crown, or short layered hair, or a mixture of the two, did not dictate a fixed form for hats. The prevailing mood of post-revolutionary Europe favoured a lack of rules and restrictions while the Napoleonic Wars, waged throughcut these years, contributed to the confusion of styles which is always a feature of war. Categories of millinery overlap and merge in confusion. The preference for small, soft shapes and the universal adoption of white muslin for dress led to the popularity of lingerie hats and bonnets, of the same materials as indoor caps but stiffened by padding or cording and made in the style of outdoor headgear. This fashion lasted until the 1840s but did not reappear again until the Edwardian period. The 'capote', a very popular style, was another example of this merging of forms, combining a soft unstructured fabric crown with a stiffened brim.

Most of the headgear of these years reflected one or other of the leading artistic or political enthusiasms of the day and is perhaps best described in the light of these. The most familiar is the taste for the culture of Classical Greece and Rome which had been the inspiration for the white muslin dress with high waist and skirt falling in clinging folds which was universally worn in these years. Since hats did not form part of Grecian female dress, the only Classical feature was the long oval caul, elongating the back of the head. The caul was based on the Greek hairstyle which enclosed the back hair in a loose cloth or net. This shape was translated best into day caps or evening head-dresses, but was occasionally seen in the crown of a capote or in a trimming of vertical bands of ribbon over a crown (see fig. 11).

Compatible with the admiration for the freedoms of the Classical world was the nostalgia for the simplicities of rural life. Round straw or chip hats bound close to the head with ribbon strings were

11 *Cap of plaited dark brown silk rouleaux combined with netted silk cord and silk ribbon, both in a matching shade. The broad diagonal bands and the netting give this cap the fashionable Grecian look and it would probably have been worn with evening dress, c.1812.*

called 'gipsy' or 'witches' hats and were sometimes worn with a handkerchief tied over the crown. Straw bonnets in the close or 'poke' style (the latter forming a horizontal line over the crown and projecting very far forwards, obscuring the profile) were known as 'cottage' bonnets. Straw hats were also popular in a form rather like a man's top hat, and a round beehive shape. Straw hats and bonnets of all types were considered suitable for morning and walking wear, while those in fabric were reserved for afternoon wear and the fashionable promenade. However, like the muslin dresses which usually accompanied them, they were not limited to spring and summer wear: the desired effect of artless simplicity had to be attained through gritted teeth. These morning straws were usually very simply trimmed, closely following their rustic prototype, and often the brim was left unlined. The widespread use of straw reflected the prosperity of the English straw industry, which benefitted from an embargo placed on the import of plait from Italy during the war with France. From its area of origin in the south-east Midlands, the plait trade spread to Cambridge, Middlesex and Essex during these years. Encouraged by offers of premiums by the Society of Arts for a British version of the prized leghorn straw, several manufacturers patented tools to split the native wheat straw to produce a finer material. Indeed these years of comparative isolation from French fashions demonstrate how deeply rooted was the Englishwoman's fondness for the rustic straw hat. English tourists who rushed to France after the Peace of Amiens in 1814 were caricatured as wearing long-waisted dresses accompanied by simple straw hats with low crowns and wide brims. [1]

The French armies during the Napoleonic Wars were so fertile in their invention of military headgear that all the basic forms current in European armies up to the First World War – the 'lancer cap', the Classical helmet of metal, and the 'shako' – were first adopted during this time. These dashing military styles were bound to influence fashion and the earliest examples were helmet-shaped hats with rounded crowns, often trimmed with broad ribbon passing over the head and round the chin, producing the effect of a chinstrap. The lancer cap, worn by the Polish Lancers who entered the French service in 1807, had a diamond shape at the top of the crown which was the inspiration for triangular 'trencher caps', worn chiefly with dinner dress. Many hats and bonnets had brims which curved away sharply at the side on a level with the ears, in the manner of a peak to a cap or helmet. The tall cylindrical crown of the shako was echoed in hats especially just before and after the

Battle of Waterloo.

The Romantic feeling for 'Gothic' ornament in costume which was to become especially marked after 1810 is already discernible around 1805. For contemporaries, the period had a very wide compass, including the sixteenth century and based on the very few portraits which were accessible in public and private collections. Popular hats for afternoon wear were so-called Spanish hats of velvet or satin with moderate crowns and brims turned back, ornamented with ostrich plumes, and presumably inspired by sixteenth-century portraits. 'Yeoman' hats with deep soft crowns gathered into a band or rolled brim were reminiscent of Tudor costume as perpetuated in the uniform of the Yeoman of the Guard, and accorded with costume details of similar vintage such as ruff collars and slashed sleeves. From around 1812 the Spanish hats began to be worn with evening dress, ushering in a fashion for evening or 'dress' hats which lasted until the 1850s. During this period, this fashion altered in detail according to the prevailing daytime trend, but remained faithful to a broadly sixteenth-century type, variously called 'Valois' or 'Henry IV'. Perhaps out of consideration, since they were frequently worn for dinner and to the opera, they tended to be smaller than the daytime mode, except in the late 1820s.

Renewed contact with the sources of French fashion at the end of the war introduced more formal styles with tall crowns and sprightly trimmings in the form of upstanding ribbon bows and larger artificial flowers, the whole effect described in 1815 as 'a chimney pot with a sweep's brush sticking out at the top'. [2] This signalled the beginning of a truly manic phase in female millinery which culminated in the late 1820s and early 1830s. In 1818, the brims of bonnets expanded dramatically to accommodate massed curls around the face. Between 1820 and 1825, a fashion for Marie Stuart shape of brim, either pointed in the middle exactly copying its historic prototype, or forming a wide kidney shape, temporarily subdued the rising tide in headgear. From 1825, a fashion for the Marie Stuart shape of brim, either pointed in the middle exactly copying its historic prototype, or forming a wide kidney shape, temporarily subdued the rising tide in headgear. Artificial flowers were placed at the summit of the head and wired to stand erect. At the extreme point of this development, in 1827 to 1830, hats tended to oust bonnets and grew widthways, unfettered by ribbon strings, which were left hanging like streamers on the shoulders. Not only the size of hats but also their decoration was at its most exuberant in these

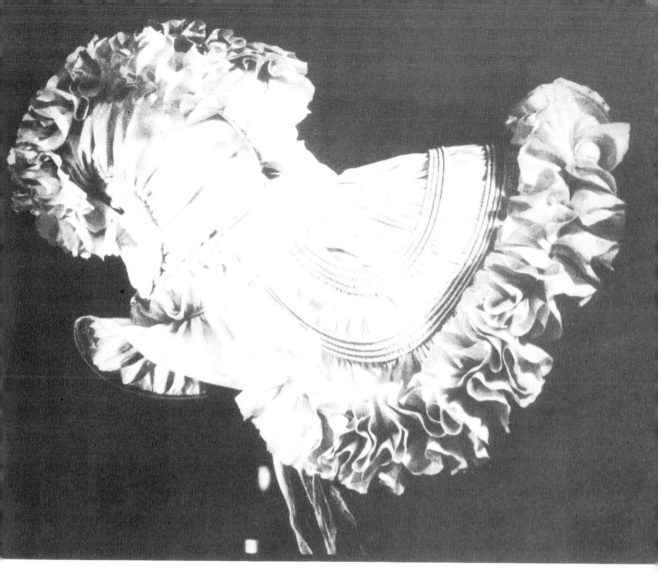

years, with loops of very wide ribbon wired to stand upright in the manner of the Apollo knot and piped and strapped rouleaux of fabric, similar to those used on the hems and sleeves of dresses, placed across brims and crowns usually in a diagonal line. This diagonal was part of a general trend towards asymmetry: the side curls were usually dressed fuller on the right side of the face and the hat was first tilted in this direction and later made wider in the brim on this side. During these years the exotic shrubs now so familiar in English country-house gardens were newly introduced following expeditions to North America and the East, and whole branches of hydrangeas, peonies and magnolia were put at the summit of hats. Similarly, exotic birds, chiefly the bird of paradise, were used as decoration (see fig. 14). The turbans which had continued as an evening fashion from 1798 onwards got caught up in the general afflatus and

12 This finely preserved bonnet, in cream taffeta, drawn over wires with trimmings of ruched matching fabric, demonstrates the size and exuberance of millinery fashions. 1829-31.

became huge turban-berets, projecting sharply at the sides like German caps of the sixteenth century (see fig. 14). Hats worn to dinner and the opera made no concessions over size in this period, providing obvious targets for the caricaturist.

Although swollen sleeves continued in fashion until 1835, the deflation of millinery had begun by 1832. The 'bibi' bonnet appeared in this year with a small crown placed further back on the head, and a brim descending low at the ears but open across the forehead. By 1835, the brim reared up off the face, framing it closely in a high oval, while the narrow,

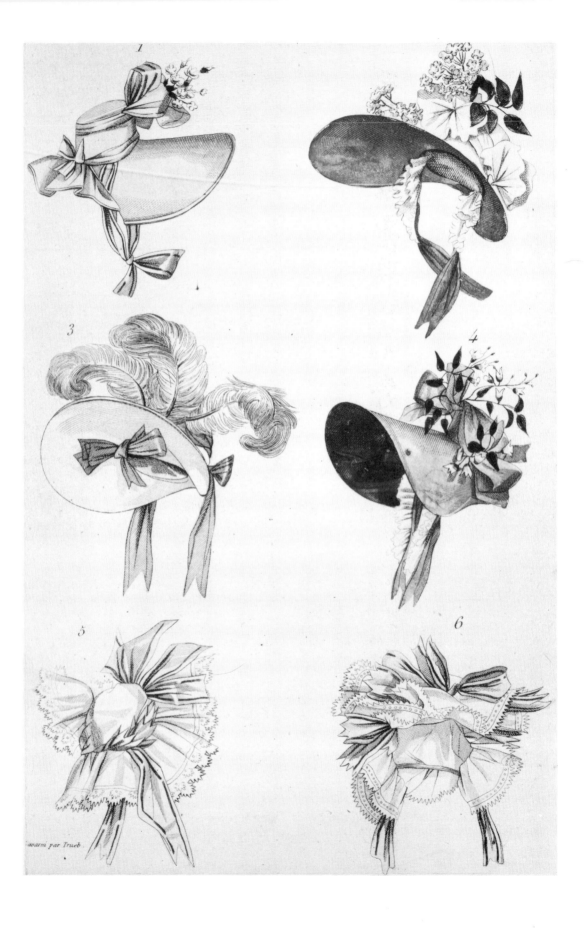

tapering crown met it at an acute angle. The new hairstyle of the second half of the 1830s was the 'Agnes Sorel' coiffure, of looped plaits or folds of hair hugging the sides of the face and concealing the ears, which is familiar from portraits of Queen Victoria on the first coinage of her realm. Also due for modest concealment was the back of the neck which was increasingly shaded by a frill of material known as a bavolet. There was no longer any room for the indoor caps which had been worn under morning bonnets since the eighteenth century. The lace edge of these caps was transferred to the inside of the bonnet immediately next to the face, and artificial flowers were added, generally on a level with the cheeks. This frame was an increasingly important piece of flattery for the face, since make-

14   Turban-beret in white silk gauze figured in coral and pale blue, mounted on a band of plaited satin rouleaux in toning colours. Trimmed white osprey feathers and white, coral and blue figured satin ribbon. This style was popular as an evening head-dress in 1826-30, especially for the married woman. This more structured form of the turban has survived better than earlier 19th century versions which were often flimsy, improvised creations.

◁ *13   Fashion plate drawn by Gavarni, 1830-32, showing the use of realistic-looking flowering shrubs as a trimming for bonnets.*

up in the form of rouge was another casualty of the new mood of prudery. By 1837 the bonnet brim had developed a downward curve at the chin edge and two years later the brims met together at the chin forming a complete circle so that the face appeared as if served up on a plate.

By 1840 the close-fitting bonnet had ousted all other styles for daytime wear. In that year, the crown and brim merged together in a single horizontal line. The fixity of form in millinery throughout this

15 *Fashion plate from the* Ladies' Magazine, *1834.* ▷
*This helpfully depicts both the front and back view
of the outfit, clearly explaining the compressed angle
between crown and brim in the fashionable 'bibi'
bonnet. The flower decoration is still mounted high
in the manner of the 1820s but the brim has become
oval.*

decade is remarkable and does not occur again until
the 1920s. Writers of fashion notes in ladies, magazines
whose predecessors earlier in the century had been at
a loss to describe the variety of styles were forced to
admit that the only variations consisted in the relat-
ively open or closed forms of the brim, the former
producing more of a circular, and the latter more of
an oval, frame to the face. [3] The early years of Queen
Victoria's reign saw the triumph of modest domestic
virtue, as exemplified in the sovereign's own family
life, and was also a time of great political unrest. In
the face of revolutions abroad and Chartist riots
at home, the wealthy fashionables evidently decided
to keep what is now known as a 'low profile'. In
keeping with this new spirit, materials and trimmings
observed a proper distinction of seasons with straw
now confined to morning wear from April to September only — the beginnings of the tradition of an
Easter bonnet. The Free Trade policy introduced in
1842 admitted a new rival to the home straw plait
industry in the form of Swiss straw braid, which
became extremely popular during the 1840s and
early 50s. The Swiss straw industry had also flourished
during the Napoleonic Wars, and the area where
plaiting had long been carried on as a seasonal cottage
industry became organized as the Canton of Aargau.
The new canton developed a rye straw, darker in
colour than wheat straw and much finer, which was
further split and flattened. Around 1840 a machine
was introduced which could twist two pieces of straw
to produce in effect a stranded yarn. This was then
used in braiding machines adapted from the textile
industry to produce delicate lace — like braids, sometimes in combination with horsehair or cotton thread.
The industry also produced charming flower and leaf
ornaments stamped out on a canvas backing, and
straw beads and tassels, so that an entire bonnet
could be assembled of straw materials (see plate 3).

For afternoon wear, the drawn bonnet is especially
characteristic of this decade and was reserved for the

16 *Bonnet covered in acid green silk with toning* ▷
ribbons in figured gauze. Height: 13½ in, c. 1838.

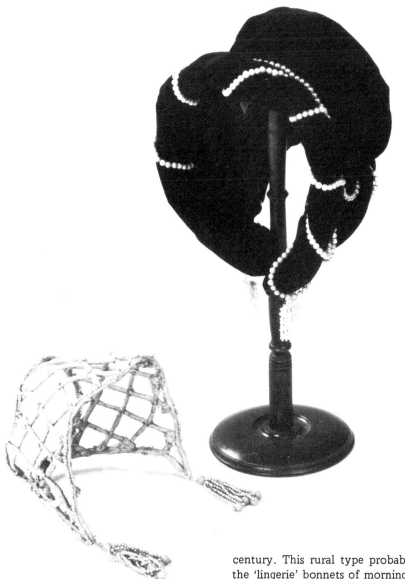

17 Two charming examples of the taste for
mediaeval-style evening head-dresses, 1836-42. Left,
wire framework covered with pale blue satin and
trimmed artificial pearls. Right, black velvet Tudor-
style bonnet, also trimmed with pearls.

most formal occasions. The material was ruched
directly on to the whalebone or cane which formed
the framework of the bonnet. This method of construction, which was used from the 1820s, has
survived in the rural sunbonnet, ruched over piping
cords, which was to be a distinctive feature of country
wear from around the 1840s until the end of the

century. This rural type probably also derives from
the 'lingerie' bonnets of morning wear which made a
similar use of cording. Trimmings on afternoon
bonnets of the 1840s usually followed the downward
drooping lines of the fashionable ringlets and featured
sprays of flowers or the weeping plumage of the bird
of paradise, placed over the crown.

Evening hats of the 1840s were rather more ad-
venturous and the Valois type of dress hat was trans-
formed by the more precise historicism of the period.
A variety of small hats and caps known as 'petits
bords', based fairly closely on mediaeval styles, were
fashionable with evening dress in the late 1830s, and
early 1840s, with the result that ladies in the satin
and tulle dresses conventional in the early Victorian
ballroom showed heads convincingly arrayed as
Marie Stuart or La Reine d'Espagne.

4

Women's Hats 1850-1900

The poke bonnet which had dominated the 1840s survived into the first two years of the new decade. During 1848-52 its appearance resembled that of the late 1830s, with the wide bonnet strings tied to the very ends of the bonnet brims, isolating the face from the rest of the costume. The effect was more startling this time, since during the 1850s the colour of the bonnet often constrasted strongly with that of the dress.[1] The shape of the brim was a sideways oval, where in the 1840s it had been upright, since the side hair was now puffed out over the ears, leaving them exposed. The effect can clearly be seen in the paintings of the Pre-Raphaelite School (see fig. 32). In 1852 the 'Eugénie' hairstyle appeared whereby the

18 *Two round hats. Left, in dark brown split plait with toning velvet ribbons forming a ruched band over the crown and hanging streamers. Right, in natural wholestraw plait. Both 1855-7, the example on the left is very close to those depicted as nos. 2 & 3 in fig. 19.*

side hair was rolled back from the centre parting, which pushed the brim of the bonnet back from the forehead. A popular version of this new style was made entirely of overlapping layers of gathered ribbon and lace, satirized by *Punch* in 1853 as resembling an oyster shell when seen from the back. This style paralleled the layers of frills also to be seen on skirts and jacket bodices. What was left of the brim tended to rise at an ever sharper angle to the face, this tendency culminating in the 'spoon' bonnet of 1860-65 which created a large gap between brim and head often to be filled in with flowers and 'high-pleached bowers of foliage'. [2] Around 1857 the back hair began to be dressed in a loose chignon rather than a bun, a change which was reflected in the 'fanchon' style, lasting into the early 1860s. This gave the effect of a sloping line over the back of the head, either by means of a long, pouched fabric caul, gathered beneath the chignon, or a hanging curtain of material attached to the crown. The fanchon echoed the line of the skirt which was distended at the back by an oval-shaped crinoline frame.

In 1865 the shape of the chignon changed again, being worn high on the crown of the head and dressed much fuller, often using artificial hair. The milliners' answer to this was the tiny 'Empire' bonnet, worn on the flat of the head stopping short of the swell of the chignon. The latter grew ever larger while bonnets had diminished by 1868 to a mere circle of material. While they lessened in size, they also threatened to become invisible as increasingly light and delicate materials were used in their construction (see plate 4). Ruched silk net, lace and crêpe made them sometimes difficult to distinguish from the dress caps which enjoyed a revival for evening wear during the 1860s. A particularly characteristic trimming, enchancing this effect of fairy-like delicacy, were the blown glass dewdrops used to edge brims and form centres to flowers — glitter powder dusted onto leaves is a similar example.

By the end of the 1860s, the bonnet had taken on a sober aspect, becoming the proper costume for the unmarried woman on formal occasions, especially church-going, and for the older married woman at all times. The centre of the stage during the late 1850s and 60s was dominated by the reappearance of the hat.

---

19 Cartoon from Punch, *22 September 1855. The streamers which floated behind these hats were christened 'follow-me-lads', while the string attached to the front brim and held in the hand was necessary to prevent the wide brim flapping in a stiff sea breeze.* ▷

THE ROUND HAT.

1. When it is all very well.   2. When it is objectionable.
3. When the Police ought to interfere.

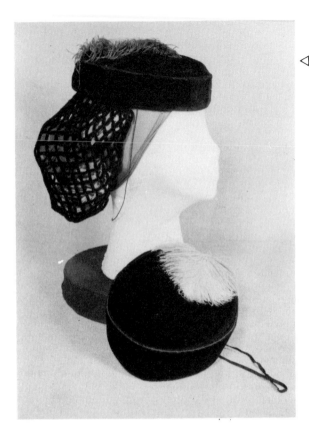

From 1855 until the advent of the crinoline frame in 1857 *Punch* is full of cartoons showing the round hats which proliferated like mushrooms on English beaches and in the countryside during these years (see fig. 19). These hats had large, down-turned brims and were usually made of brown or dark-coloured straw, simply trimmed with ribbon bands and streamers. By 1857 this style had been modified into a smaller version with dipped front brim and feather plume which was more widely adopted as a riding and walking hat. In 1859 the 'pork pie' hat appeared,

21 'The Travelling Companions', by Augustus Egg, c.1860. Sisters, even grown-up ones, were often dressed alike in upper-class families. These girls have matching grey silk travelling dresses and pork pie hats in dark straw. The landscape seen through the window of their private carriage suggests the south of France.
▽

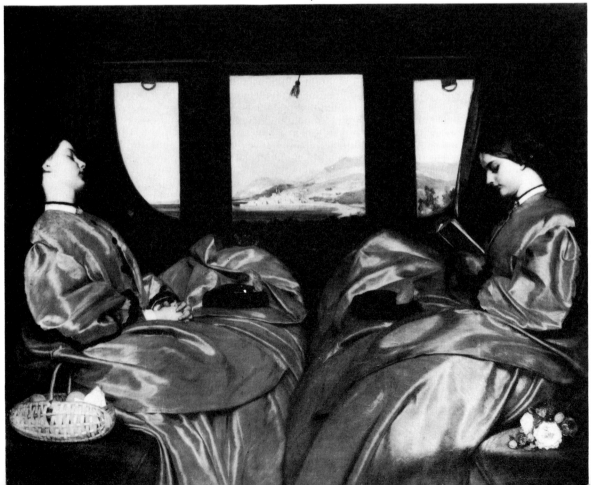

SOMETHING MORE APROPOS OF BLOOMERISM.

(BEHIND THE COUNTER THERE IS ONE OF THE "INFERIOR ANIMALS.")

also in dark straw or velvet, trimmed with a small feather. These simple styles, considerably less dramatic than the hat in its last fashionable appearance in the 1830s, caused great controversy among contemporaries, which seems rather puzzling to us. The wearers, usually young girls during the 1850s, were frequently referred to as 'fast young ladies'. We have seen that the wide-brimmed straw hat of rustic origin was a persistent feature of Englishwomen's dress in the eighteenth and nineteenth centuries. The shepherdess hat of the mid-eighteenth century survived as the gipsy hat of the early nineteenth century. Even in the period from 1820-50 it was retained on the fringes of

22 Cartoon from Punch, 1851. All of the many jokes in Punch about the followers of the American dress reformer, Mrs Bloomer, depict them wearing wide-brimmed straw hats of the type which was to become popular in the mid-century. However, in 1851-2, Bloomerism does not appear to have attracted many converts in England.

fashion for country wear and in the dress of small children. In the vocabulary of female headgear the wide-brimmed straw hat stood for emancipation and this was well understood in the climate of the 1850s.

When the American Amelia Bloomer devised her famous costume (which was first seen in England in 1851-2) she selected the features of contemporary informal dress which seemed to her most rational — the wide straw hat, and the jacket — to accompany her Turkish trousers. This headgear, ridiculed when worn by the Bloomers in 1851, was essentially the same as appeared on entirely conventional heads at the English seaside four years later.

Political emancipation for women was in its infancy in the 1860s, but physical and social emancipation was an outstanding feature of this decade. The development of the seaside was a great forcing ground for informal fashions. On the crowded beaches class barriers were broken down, yet, unlike the country, the proximity of contemporaries and possible suitors stimulated the desire for display. Margate had been accessible to the London masses by steamer from Gravesend since the 1830s, but it was the boom in excursion travel by railway in the 1850s which really launched the seaside holiday. At the seaside the Victorian girl could quite literally let her hair down: with the pork pie hats popular in the early 1860s crocheted nets were worn to hold the hair which was more formally dressed in a chignon. By the mid-1860s, the hair was worn completely loose, hanging down the back to the waist.[3] The hats which accompanied this style were variations on two new male styles, the bowler and the boater, both made with much shallower, oval-shaped crowns. The same freedoms and the same hat styles were permissable on the croquet lawns, since this genteel game, launched in the 1860s, was actually the first of the new sports for women.

In the course of the 1860s the boundaries of the English middle classes expanded even further. From railway excursions to the seaside in the 50s Thomas Cook progressed to organizing the foreign tours

23 Flat hats based on the traditional peasant head-gear of the south of France. Left, straw trimmed pale blue velvet and artificial flowers with matching bow and hanging ends on an elastic cord, designed to tilt the hat over the forehead. Right, straw and cotton weave, trimmed ruched white muslin and black velvet. Diameter: 10 in. Both hats 1868-70.

24 'The Newest Fashions for Spring and Summer ▷ hats', from the Englishwoman's Domestic Magazine, *May 1869. The caption informs us that 'The models of the bonnets illustrated may be seen and purchased at Madame Parson's, Marchande de Modes, 92, Regent Street and 26-27 & 37-38 Burlington Arcade'. The hat in the top centre is similar to those in fig. 23.*

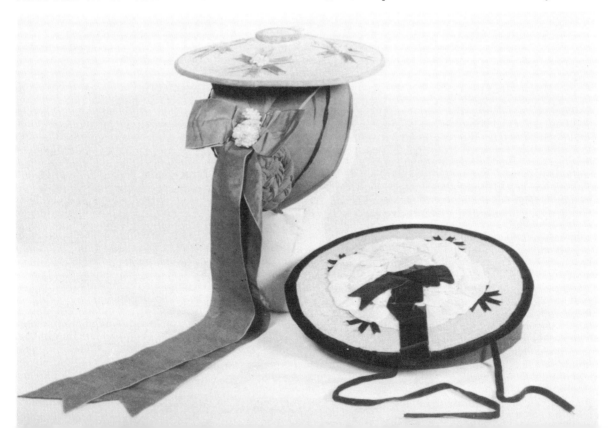

THE NEWEST FASHIONS FOR SPRING AND SUMMER BONNETS AND HATS
Expressly designed for the "Englishwoman's Domestic Magazine"

GREAT SHOW OF CHIGNONS.
A HINT FOR THE HAIRDRESSERS' SOCIETY

with which his name is associated. The popular venues were Switzerland and the south of France, both established earlier in the century as upper-class playgrounds. Both these areas were to influence the fashion for hats, which was well established by the second half of the decade and extended to older married women. Flat straw hats with crossed decorations of velvet ribbon were popular at the end of the 60s and were based on the traditional peasant style of the French Riviera (see fig. 23). They were worn tilted over the forehead above the rising chignon which we have noted as the cause of the shrinking of the bonnet at this time. The Swiss and Austrian Alps influenced the Tyrolean style of crown, tapering upwards and sometimes with a shallower slope at the back than the front. This crown is found in a low form from the mid-1860s and became much higher at the end of the decade and into the 70s.

The closing years of the 1860s and early years of the 70s were dominated by a revival of the styles of exactly one hundred years earlier. The flat 'Niçoise' (south of France) hats were variations on a 'Bergère' style which was bound to the sides of the head with

25 Punch cartoon, 21 July 1866. As the chignon grew in size, the bonnet retreated into the tiny 'Empire' shape. Hats of the bowler type were very much shallower than in the early 1860s.

ribbon and tilted forwards over the enormous chignons of mostly false hair. These were worn with 'polonaise' gowns and the whole ensemble was called a 'Dolly Varden' after the heroine of Charles Dickens's novel *Barnaby Rudge*, set in the 1770s. By 1874 the hairdressing had subsided to a more modest 'catagan' coiffure, a chignon hanging down to the nape of the neck, and the bonnet had established a new angle which it kept until the end of the 1880s: an oval shaped crown with small or minimal brim worn at a diagonal line over the back of the head, exposing the fringe at the front and nesting securely over the curls or knot of hair on the crown.

By the closing years of the 1870s a new variety of form and complexity of trimmings was noticeable in hats, reflecting a trend which lasted throughout the

1880s. The leading artistic influence of this time was the Aesthetic movement, really a late phase of Pre-Raphaelitism with the focus on reform in the decorative, rather than the fine arts. Although intended as what would now be called an 'alternative culture', its concern with the minor arts of life lay so close to the roots of fashion that it tended to become enmeshed with some very conventional aspects of society in that decade. The colours advocated by the movement had an immediate effect on fashionable dress and hats, substituting autumnal tones of rust, sage green and slate grey, accented with metallic bronze and steel, for the clear primaries of the 1860s and early 1870s. The women belonging to the inner clique of Aesthetes modelled their dress closely on Old Master paintings, but the popular aspect of this was a more muddled historicism. The popular 'Gainsborough' hat, of velvet or plush, the brim turned up at one side or at the front, and simply trimmed with ostrich feathers, was actually closer to the familiar sixteenth century or 'Rubens' type. However, the 'Directoire' revival, which began in the late 1870s

and continued with differing emphasis until the First World War, had a more profound influence on millinery. This taste was related to the Aesthetic movement since leading figures like Kate Greenaway and Walter Crane depicted people in the dress of the late eighteenth or early nineteenth centuries — the period encompassed in the term 'Directoire'. The small straw bonnets of the 1880s did resemble the styles of this period as seen through the eyes of contemporary artists. Another form taken by the Directoire revival in millinery from around 1884 to 1886 was a hat with tall, rigid tapering crown and shallow brim, often decorated with cockades and loops of riboon, the whole very close to that actually worn after the Revolution in France, and accompanied by appropriately striped costumes. Its popular name was 'three storeys and a basement' or the 'post boy' hat, after the style which replaced the top hat in the postal service from 1862. These tall-crowned hats of the mid-1880s were sometimes made with a brim shape which was a true innovation of the decade, the 'gable', rising sharply to a point at front and back. A further Directoire style appeared at the very end of the 80s and continued into the 90s: a flat-crowned hat or bonnet with deep brim projecting at the front only, based on the poking hat of the 1790s.

Another feature of the Aesthetic movement was its search for greater truth to nature, a thread which ran throughout nineteenth-century art, but in the 1880s took the form of a particular delight in those

26 Green velvet hat in the form of a Tudor flat cap, 1892-1900. Labelled 'Liberty & Co. Artistic and Historic Costume Studio, 222, Regent Street'. Liberty moved to Regent Street in 1892 and continued to provide 'artistic' styles in millinery for their customers until well into the 20th century.

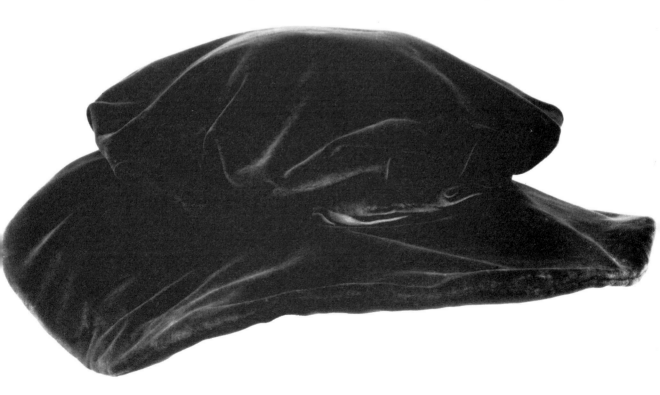

aspects of nature which would commonly be rejected as unpicturesque. The 1880s and 90s were the heyday of the commercial development of the art of taxidermy which had been developing since the middle of the century among collectors and sportsmen. This craft perfectly combined the artistic, sporting and scientific interests of the later nineteenth century with that unconscious element of the bizarre which is such a marked feature of the 1880s. Its development parallels and helps to explain some of the more extraordinary trends in millinery in this decade. Its most obvious relationship to hats was in the enormous popularity of birds' plumage as a trimming. This began in the 1860s with the use of a single feather or small wing on the new hat styles and by the end of the decade the bird's head was often included along with the plumage. By the the late 1870s and early 1880s whole birds were frequently used, along with

---

27 The last stages of the bonnet. Left, black net machine-embroidered in coloured metallic threads and trimmed ostrich feathers and French jet. Labelled 'C. & D. Milliners, Cooperative Society, Luton Rd., Chatham'. Worn by a lady for her silver wedding celebrations in 1911. Right, black fancy straw, satteen ribbons, pink artificial flowers and black glass beads. Labelled 'Mrs. J. Furlong, Milliner and Ladies Outfitter, 61, North Street, Guildford'. Worn by a housemaid for church going on Sundays, 1890-95.

small stuffed animals such as mice and reptiles. The latter were used as trimming for toques of velvet or sealskin.[4] (The toque became established in this period as the safe and tasteful choice for all but the most dressy occasions, a role it kept until the First World War.) There was also a fondness for insects, either real or in the form of jewelled pins. The increased popularity of birds' plumage led to the growth of a lucrative worldwide trade of which London was the auction mart and involved the slaughter of countless rare birds. Already by 1889 the Society for the Protection of Birds had been formed in protest, but the trade continued to prosper and the great heyday of plumage in millinery was to be in the Edwardian period.

The concern of artistic taxidermists in the 1880s was to provide their clients not only with well-mounted specimens but to set them within an accurate and realistic natural setting. This involved the gathering and treating of real moss, leaves, etc. Millinery trimmings took a similarly realistic turn with the emphasis on the rank and decaying aspects of nature. Worm-eaten autumn leaves, faded field flowers were all recommended by fashionable magazines[5] and were cleverly copied in cloth and wire. By the end of the decade real twigs, grasses and mosses were featured on hats.[6] Some highly fashionable bonnets of the 1880s formed miniature habitat groups and were some of the most extraordinary creations in nineteenth-century millinery (see plate 5). Even on more conventional examples the complexity of trimming was remarkable, with lace, embroidery, flowers and feathers all combined on one small bonnet.

The foundation of many bonnets in the 80s was a coarse straw plait known as 'rustic'. Straw hats and bonnets were worn at all seasons, as they had been in the early nineteenth century, and were worn with some unlikely outfits — they accompanied bathing costumes from the late 1870s and were adopted by the police of Luton with their summer uniforms around the same date. This widespread use reflected an expansion in the English straw industry. The first machine widely used in the industry to sew straw plait was the '10 guinea' machine issued in 1875. Also in the 70s machine blocking was introduced, and straw plait began to be imported from China at about a quarter of the price of the English product. After

1891, Japan also began to export plait. These imports gradually killed the straw-plaiting industry in Bedfordshire, but created a boom for the manufacturing side. During the 1880s, working women were able to keep pace with millinery fashions as never before, and Flora Thompson has recorded how the post boy fashion came and went in her Oxfordshire village.[7]

The great triumph of this phase of the straw industry was the boater which was worn from 1884 and increasingly until the end of the century. It was the sporting hat par excellence, being worn for tennis, cycling, boating and spectator sports. The 1880s saw a great expansion in the variety of sports open to women, and consequent variety of styles of sporting hat. The 'tam-o'-shanter', the 'peaked cap' and the 'deerstalker' were all worn for sports and country wear. Felt hats were more widely worn by women for these activities after felt hat manufacture was introduced to Luton in the 1870s.

The unconscious surrealism of the 1880s merged into the cultivated strangenesses of the 'fin de siècle' in the 90s, also providing a fertile field for millinery. Particularly characteristic of this decade was the imaginative combination of materials and colours. Chenille was combined with raffia to make a fancy straw,[8] black wire mesh with real moss and flowers,[9] chinchilla fur with artificial violets. Straw was dyed in very bright colours and light materials were often bordered with dark, especially on brims. There was also a tendency to contrast in form: bonnets became very small and were called 'dolls' hats' while hats by the middle of the decade had become very wide in the brim. The crowns of hats rose from 1893 to 1898 and a variety of novelty shapes were tried: sugarloaf, hour glass and witch's crown. The homburg shape of crown became popular for sporting wear. Trimmings emphasized height with Prince of Wales feathers, lace aigrettes and mercury wings. Consistent to hats and bonnets was the angle, absolutely straight on the head. In the last three years of the decade wide-brimmed hats such as the new 'toreador' shape were worn with a forwards or sideways tilt and the popularity of tulle and chiffon trimmings also looked forward to the Edwardian style. Younger women abandoned the bonnet and its final ignominy came in the early years of the next century when it was relegated to a special section in trade catalogues headed 'Old Ladies' and Nurses' Bonnets'.[10]

5
Men's Hats 1800-1900

The life cycle of the top hat in the nineteenth century followed very closely the one we have traced for the bonnet: both were born at the very end of the eighteenth century, reached a peak of dominance in mid century and encountered challenge from other styles, surviving in a modified form until the end of the century.

For the first forty years of the century the top hat held absolute sway over men's daytime headgear. There was some variety in form: up to 1810 crowns

28 *Group of men standing by the* Leviathan *steamship, American photograph of the 1850s. Contemporary records such as these remind us that top hats were standard wear for working and formal occasions alike during the 1840s and 1850s.*

29 Top hats, 1830-1900, showing relative sizes and shapes. Left, black beaver felt, 'stove pipe' shape of crown, c.1850. Height: 7¼ in (compare fig. 30). Centre, black silk plush, worn as a best wear hat in the 1830s by the driver of London-Worthing coach. Modified Wellington style of crown, labelled 'W. Roberts'. Height: 6¼ in. Right, black silk plush with cloth mourning band, c.1890. Height: 7 in, 2½ in band.

WHICH LOOKS THE MOST RIDICULOUS?

30 Punch cartoon, 1853. This satirizes the tall-crowned, narrow-brimmed masculine top hat and off-the-face female bonnet.

and brims both tended to be broad, while the 'Wellington' shape with concave sides to the crown was popular in the 1820s and 30s when its curves echoed the rounded lapels and padded 'pouter pigeon' chests of the currently fashionable frock coat. In the 1830s the 'Cumberland' hat, tall and narrowing towards the top, resembled the tapered crowns of women's hats and bonnets in this decade. A very short version was worn throughout this period and became identified with the yeoman farmer — we are familiar with it as part of the dress of 'John Bull'. Even very small boys, aged three or four, wore the top hat up to 1820, when a variety of caps, similar to the forage caps of military wear, came into fashion. These always had a leather peak and sometimes a tassel, and were frequently depicted in Phiz's illustrations to the early novels of Charles Dickens. They were also worn by very young men, but for their elders there was no equivalent informal fashion.

The evening dress hat which was correct wear until 1840 was, like the knee breeches worn with it, a survivor from the daytime wear of the late eighteenth century. This was the 'opera hat', a collapsible form of the bicorne, with a soft crown and rigid sides which formed a complete crescent shape, and was always carried, not worn. The first collapsible form of the top hat appeared in 1812, and was followed by

31 *Carte-de-visite photograph, c.1860s. Etiquette demanded that men take off their hats but keep them by their sides when paying social calls (see 'The Etiquette of the Hat' at the end of this book).*

cricketers and policemen all go about their occupations wearing top hats. The top hat reached its most extreme form at this time, the crown being the highest in the century and the brim narrowest, emphasizing its vertical quality (see fig. 30). A variety with totally straight sides was given the name of 'stove pipe' while that with slightly convex sides was known as the 'chimney pot'. During the early part of the century beaver felt had gradually been superseded by silk 'hatter's plush' as the chief material for the top hat, so that by 1850 its dark lustrous surface symbolized the respect in which it was held. Already in its moment of triumph during the 1850s there were voices of protest raised against the top hat from artists and intellectuals and by the late 1870s even the trade journals of the hatting industry carried frequent articles heralding the end of the fashion. [1] Yet the top hat has proved to be the most obstinate hat type yet devised, still surviving today for limited ceremonial use after nearly two hundred years. The truth is that by the time the Industrial Revolution was well under way in the 1840s the top hat had changed from a fashion to a symbol. It stood for urban respectability and the less well-to-do would hire toppers, buy second-hand ones or cheap versions made of papier maché in order to bear this proof of gentility. In addition, from the mid-1840s social changes were giving rise to a variety of informal fashions which by 1870 had established themselves as an alternative to the top hat except for the most formal daytime and evening wear.

The two informal styles of hat which emerged in the late 1840s and early 1850s were the straw hat and the soft felt hat. Both sprang from truly popular roots and for this reason the influences which shaped the fashion are difficult to pinpoint. Certainly the evidence for male fashions at this time is very different from the picture of staid respectability which is the stereotype for the Victorian male. Enormous propeller-shaped cravats, 'peg-top' trousers with huge windowpane checks, brocade waistcoats and shirts with novelty patterns of horses' heads and dancers, can only be described as 'loud'. These jolly, vulgar aspects were part of a truly democratic trend in men's wear which led to the adoption of the loose lounge jacket into men's wardrobes in the 50s, the forerunner of the modern lounge suit.

The first of these informal styles, the straw hat, is the easier to account for. Straw versions of the top hat had occasionally been adopted for summer wear in the early nineteenth century, but the fashion never became widespread. In 1846 *Punch* depicted men on the steamers bound for Margate wearing straw hats

various improved patents for 'elastic' hats, culminating in the 'gibus' of 1840. The latter was made of corded silk or cloth over a metal framework which sprung open with a flick of the wrist. These and the ordinary rigid form of the top hat were carried with less formal evening wear from the 1820s, and the bicorne was ousted altogether by 1840.

The 1840s and early 1850s saw the heyday of the top hat. The increased variety of informal headgear which was to emerge by the 1860s was still in its formative stages, while industrial prosperity was bringing fashionable clothing within reach of a much wider section of the population. The new medium of photography has put on record an England where workmen constructing the roof of the Crystal Palace, railway engineers, shepherds in smock frocks,

similar to those worn with sailors' uniforms at this
date. In the same year, Winterhalter had depicted the
Prince of Wales in the miniature sailor's uniform,
complete with straw hat, which he had worn aboard
the Royal Yacht. [2] To the influence of the seaside
and of patriotism can be added that of the United
States, which first affected men's wear around this

*32 'The Last of England', by Ford Madox Brown,
1852-5. This painting depicts a family emigrating
to Australia. The man wears a felt 'wideawake' hat
secured by a string to his buttonhole. His wife's
bonnet shows the elliptical shape of the very early
1850s.*

ON THE BOULOGNE PIER.
(TWO ASIDES.)

Young England. "RUMMY STYLE OF 'AT!"   *La Jeune France.* "DRÔLE DE CHAPEAU!"

33 Punch *cartoon, 8 September 1866. The short style of top hat, nicknamed the 'Muller-cut-down', seems to have been an English fashion which did not catch on in France.*

---

time. Straw hats were a regular part of men's dress in the United States, especially the Southern States, and a wide-brimmed straw known as a 'Jim Crow' was part of the contemporary English caricature of a 'Yankee'.

The seaside was also the stage for the development of the second informal fashion, the round felt hat. Frith's *Ramsgate Sands* (1851-2)[3] depicts most of the men on the beach wearing felt hats with wide brims and soft, unstiffened crowns. These were known as 'wideawakes' (according to *Punch*, 'because they have no nap' — they were made of hard felt rather than hatter's plush). During the 1840s and 50s cab and onmibus drivers had worn a felt hat with stiff, rounded crown usually topped with a button, and known as a 'bollinger'. This stiffened version of the round felt hat was soon adopted in progressive circles — Prince Albert was photographed holding one in 1854[4] — and by the 1860s was widely fashionable under the name of a 'bowler'. The leading hatter and hat manufacturer at this time claimed direct responsibility for the invention of the stiff and soft versions

respectively of the round felt hat. Lock's of St James's Street have records of a commission undertaken in 1850 to provide a hard-crowned felt as an alternative to the top hat for the gamekeepers of William Coke of Holkham, Norfolk. They devised a model based on the round riding hats of the 1780s and the prototype was made in co-operation with William Bowler & Co. of Southwark, their regular suppliers of felt hoods. When the hat was put into wider production, it was known both as a 'Coke' and a 'Bowler'.[5] A confusion has arisen over this story because of the resemblance of the two terms 'Bullycock' (given to the aristocratic 'bullies' of the 1730s who affected slouched hats) and 'Billycock' (a name given in the later nineteenth century to a version of the wideawake worn by labourers) to the name of William Coke. Similarly the firm of T. W. Christy and Co. claimed that the invention of the wideawake was made in 1842 when a representative of the firm visited the estate of Aveley, found the top hats worn by the workers unsuitable, and devised a less rigid alternative.[6] These stories all point in one direction: the round felt hat obviously supplied a deep-felt need in the mid-nineteenth century and the form it took was a deliberate throwback to the last appearance of the round hat in the late eighteenth century. The need for a more democratic alternative to the top hat had long been felt by artists and intellectuals, and French bohemian artists of the 1830s and 40s had worn dark felt hats with wide drooping brims, probably inspired by the hats depicted in seventeenth-century portraits by Van Dyck and Rembrandt. The young Pre-Raphaelites from 1848 and Whistler in the 1850s continued this tradition. Similar hats were worn by the Hungarian revolutionary Louis Kossuth who visited New York in 1851 and by Liszt two years later, when he aroused the suspicion of the police for wearing a 'democratic' hat.[7]

A wide variety of informal headgear was characteristic of the 1860s. To the two forms of the round hat were added the straw or felt pork pie and the velvet 'glengarry'. In mid-decade, the top hat developed a new, short-crowned variation, which became known as the 'Muller-cut-down' since the murderer of that name was identified in 1865 by his wearing of this headgear (see fig. 33). In the same year, the Duke of Cambridge asked Lock's to produce a flat-crowned version of the bowler which remained popular as a 'Cambridge' until the Great War. The Tyrolean style which was a short-lived fashion for

34 Photograph, 1885-90. The sitter wears a light coloured felt trilby with ribbon bound brim. The crowns of all types of hat tended to be high in the 1880s.

women in the late 1860s and early 1870s had a more profound effect on men's headgear. The Prince of Wales sported an Alpine hat with tapered crown and curled brim on visits to the spar at Homburg in the 60s, and these features were given to felt hats in the 70s which were later known as 'trilbys'.[8] Also new in the 1870s were two hats of tropical origin, the 'panama' from Central America and the 'helmet' hat based on the Indian 'sola topi'. The helmet hat had a limited popularity for summer wear and was still unusual enough in the 1890s to cause Mr Pooter's son Lupin to refuse to accompany his father on the promenade while he was wearing 'a hat in the shape of the helmet worn in India, only made of straw'.[9] The Aesthetic movement had a very limited effect on men's fashion. In 1880 Henry Heath advertised 'Ye Olde Englishe Hatte' for sports wear. This was a very supple felt which had lasting popularity as a folding or 'pocket' hat for travelling. Oscar Wilde ordered a 'velvet hat' from Lock's for his lecture tour of the United States in the 1880s, which may have been based on the pouched tam-o'-shanter style satirized in Patience. This survived as a fashion for women, not men. A marked feature of bowlers and soft felts in the 1880s was the height of the crown, which kept pace with the rising trend in women's hats (see fig. 34).

The true conservatism of men's fashions so often credited to the whole nineteenth century truly belonged to the last quarter only. All the major hat styles which have lasted into our own century have their origin in the fertile period of social change from c.1848-70. During the 1880s and 90s no new styles were added which had any lasting popularity, the only changes being in detail and emphasis. The boater, the soft felt and the bowler all became acceptable for town wear with a lounge suit in the 1880s, leaving the top hat as the only acceptable accompaniment to the frock coat and the tail coat. In the 1890s, the typical form of the top hat was slim, neat and waisted, words which could also be used to describe the fashionable line in men's tailoring during this decade. The wide-awake went down the social scale from the 1870s and was worn by labourers as a 'billycock'. The bowler tended to become the 'best hat' of the working man. For the rest of the century and up to the Great War, men's hats were an index of social class as never before or since. Flora Thompson, describing villagers going to church in the 1880s, noted that the 'squire and the farmers wore top hats and the squire's head gardener and the schoolmaster and village carpenter. The farm labourers wore bowlers or the older men, soft round black felts'.[10]

6

Women's Hats 1900-1920

The first four years of the new century saw a definite Art Nouveau feeling in millinery. Movement was the key to the style. Brims were always curved, often on either side of the centre front in a variation of the tricorne or Marquise style. During the first two years, the front brim often curved upwards and projected forward, giving the effect of a boat's prow. Sometimes the brim rippled throughout and a characteristically organic form consisted of overlapping layers of tucked tulle on an undulating wire foundation, the whole resembling a giant oyster shell. In addition to their shape, the angle of these hats on the head was frequently asymmetric, being tilted to one side or to the front.

The illusion created was of the hat floating upon the head, and this illusion extended to the shapes of the hats themselves. Hats had never before been less securely located in relation to the head and the actual shape of the hat had never been less apparent. All trimmings were swathed or puffed, especially the chiffon and tulle which enjoyed a universal sway over all aspects of dress at this date. Feathers were soft and drooping. Millinery magazines for these years illustrate the evolution of a hat from basic shape to final trimmed form, but it would be almost impossible to infer the former from the latter.[1] A popular shape of crown, tapering inwards towards the base, is nearly always obscured by trimmings. Black and white were the popular colours, combined with pastels for spring and summer and soft neutrals for winter. Ribbon trimmings, especially black velvet, were often narrow and were frequently strapped to produce a trimming also seen on dresses, the intersections marked with a diamanté bead. Black velvet was also used for 'bonnet' strings. Leghorn adapted well to undulating styles, as did crinoline, and both enjoyed a revival. Rosettes of ribbon are an example of the Directoire influence which continued to gather strength until the First World War. From 1903 the foamy illusion created by the trimmings was increased by the widespread use of large lace veils which were tied around the entire hat or later swathed around

the crown with one end falling over the shoulders. All these styles were depicted in magazines through the medium of lithography which conveyed their softness as faithfully as steel engravings had mirrored the crisp, pert effects of the late nineteenth century.

This illusion of floating in millinery was achieved by an armoury of weapons, much as pouched and fluted lines of Edwardian dresses rested on a substructure of rigid boning. The period saw another great age of the professional hairdresser, comparable with the end of the eighteenth century. In 1902 the 'Pompadour' frame appeared to support the hair, while pads made of combings from the lady's own hair (vulgarly called 'rats') and full wigs or hair pieces (politely known as 'transformations') were similar devices in the battle to gain volume and height in hairdressing (see fig. 35). Hats could rest on these supporting structures to which they could be anchored by means of hatpins, without endangering the scalp. These pins had appeared in the 1890s and were widely used only from c.1903. Between 1904 and 1907, hair and hats concentrated on height, and the width of brim was reduced. Bowlers of straw with high, round crowns were popular in 1905. Hats were worn at an extreme forward or sideways tilt, supported by 'bandeaux', the gap above the hair filled in by a 'chou' of ribbons or banked-up flower trimmings.

36 *Three ladies, 1905-6. Hats were not universally* ▷ *wide-brimmed throughout the Edwardian period; at this date they were small but trimmings emphasized height.*

44

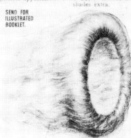

37 *Lady on a bicycle, c.1906. Flat tweed caps were worn for a variety of sports including motoring, golf and cycling.*

All the characteristics described thus far were most apparent in the 'dressy' hat. Throughout the period, small brimmed hats in felt in the toque and tricorne styles, modestly trimmed, were adopted for everyday wear, especially in winter. For these hats, stronger colour was introduced, navy, emerald and purple being fashionable in 1903 and cherry and olive in 1906. Felt homburgs, panamas and boaters were widely worn for sport, while the distinctive pancake-style motoring hat in tweed with a gored crown was introduced around 1905 and was also used for golf, and in different materials, for yachting.

Nevertheless, as the decade wore on, dressy hats in light materials were worn for an increasing variety of occasions. The nostalgic impression gained from novels and memoirs of the Edwardian period as one of endless summer is certainly borne out by millinery. Around 1904, 'lingerie' hats of embroidered muslin or lace became popular for boating and were later adopted for general summer wear. Crêpe paper hats also appeared in this way and making them became a popular hobby. Paper and lingerie hats were joined by hats smothered in 'country garden' flowers — wisteria, roses, laburnum and sweet peas. The truth was that the upper classes had secured for themselves a perpetual summer. They wintered on the Riviera or the Nile and, when at home, sporting and outdoor occasions such as garden parties were popular as never before. Society increasingly sought more public forms of entertainment. While servants were abundant, the 'best families' preferred to attend dinners and balls at each others' houses. When the servant shortage became acute in the 1890s, restaurants, hotels, theatres and casinos were widely patronized. Within these establishments showy 'toilettes' and light, elaborately trimmed millinery could be worn regardless of the time of year or time of day.

Interest in height in hairdressing had changed by 1908 to an interest in width, the hair being parted in the middle and 'teased' out at the sides over the ears. Width of brim was called for and increased dramatically towards 1910, while skirts contracted. This inverse proportion had been seen in the late eighteenth century and indeed 1910 marks the apogee of the Directoire revival, now usually called Empire. The most characteristic example of the 'big hat' phase and a truly popular millinery fashion was the 'Merry Widow' hat, actually worn by Lily Elsie in the operetta of 1907 and designed by Lucile, but influencing fashions for the next three years. The Merry Widow hat was always black, often made in a dull-surfaced straw like chip or tagel and had a deep crown which was swathed in black tulle or black ostrich feathers. It was frequently worn with a white 'lingerie' dress which emphasized its Directoire inspiration. The Merry Widow hat is the supreme instance of the influence of the stage on fashions in this period which saw the heyday of operetta and musical comedy. Actresses like Lily Elsie were the heroines

38 *Photograph of Heather Firbank, c.1910. Miss ▷ Firbank's hat has the fashionable wreath of large flowers, obscuring the crown. The actual hat is preserved in the Victoria and Albert Museum.*

39 Toque covered with cock pheasant's head and plumage, 1908-10. This was the 'best wear' hat of a lady who lived in Ipswich — the family story preserved with the hat is that the lady's husband forbade her to wear it in the country during the shooting season!

of the day and their stage outfits, frequently designed by leading London couturiers such as Lucile, were described in ladies' magazines. The great prestige of the stage at this time, combined with the public trend in entertainment noted earlier, no doubt influenced the increasingly dramatic trend in hats.

Trimmings also became huge, as if designed to 'tell' from the back of the stalls. Large flowers such as daisies, poppies and cabbage roses ringed, and frequently obscured, crowns. Hatpins came into their own as an accessory and attained lengths of up to 14 inches, with large disc-shaped heads.[2] Bolder, heavier effects were sought — corded silk was a popular covering material while a very shaggy brushed felt known as 'beaverette' was introduced for winter hats in 1909. Since hats were worn at a very straight angle and wide, mushroom-shaped crowns were popular, they were 'inclined to bury the head'.[3] As hair styles contracted into the close Empire mode, this threatened to be literally true, and bandeaux were employed to keep the hat securely anchored.[4]

Another tendency that culminated around 1910 was the love of birds' plumage as a trimming. From 1901, small toque hats had been entirely covered with game birds' feathers such as pheasant.[5] Later the stuffed head was placed on the front brim while the plumage was disposed around the crown, so that the hat had almost been metamorphosed into a bird (see fig. 39). Game and poultry feathers were not an issue with the anti-plumage lobby which we saw developing in the later years of the nineteenth century. Neither were ostrich feathers which could be

1 Mary, Countess Howe, by Thomas Gainsborough, c.1765.
The countess wears her straw hat at a very straight angle,
giving it a Chinoiserie flavour.

2   Fine silk bonnet, 1805-8. This example has the soft, close-fitting crown typical of its period. Yellow was a popular colour as it made a pleasing contrast with white muslin dresses.

3   Crinoline and straw bonnet, trimmed with silk taffeta ribbons, blonde lace and artificial flowers, 1848-52. Labelled 'Mrs. Bell, Milliner, 34, Wigmore Street, Grosvenor Square'.

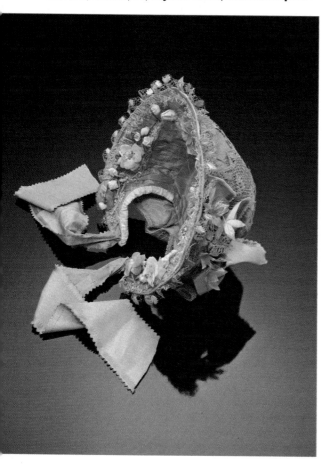

4   Bonnet of silk net and lace over a wire foundation, c.1868. The trimming of blown glass dewdrops enhances the delicacy of this bonnet.

40 *Hat woven in shaded chenille thread decorated with the head and wings of an owl, c.1912. This owl, mounted on the centre of the hat with glass eyes staring directly forward, has an alarming effect when seen today but would not have caused comment in 1912 when the wearing of all manner of stuffed birds was a long-established fashion.*

plucked from the tail feathers of the living bird without harming it. Ostriches were farmed in South Africa, North America and the south of France to supply the increased demands of the millinery trade. The problem lay in the use of 'osprey' feathers, a generic term for the feathers of rare and exotic birds such as the bird of paradise or species of the egret. While the fashion for osprey remained modest, anti-plumage agitation progressed well. In 1904 King Edward VII granted a royal charter to the SPB and two years later Queen Alexandra announced she would not wear osprey. The first Anti-Plumage Bill was launched in 1908 but failed to get through the Commons. The fact was that by this date an abundance of rare plumage on hats had become a status symbol, part of the trend towards ostentation which we have already noted. It was akin to the increased use of costly furs, such as sable and chinchilla, on every conceivable occasion, even with summer dresses. During 1908-14 magazines become silent on the plumage issue, while hats crowned with a halo of osprey and costing up to 50 guineas were sported on the fashionable race course and promenade. The battle was not won in England until after the Great War. [6]

Two new trends in 1908 which were pointers to the future were the very straight angle at which hats were worn and the new deep crowns. The latter were called variously cloches, mushrooms, beehives, thimbles, Napoleons or bicornes. All these forms had narrow brims and a trend towards even smaller hats was first seen in sports hats in this year. Close-fitting knitted turbans were introduced for skiing and the new sport of 'rinking',[7] while Victorian style motor bonnets, with puffed crowns gathered into a band at the neck, replaced the flat tweed cap. Hats were generally smaller from 1911, except for the most dressy occasions, for which the huge picture hat still survived. Small stitched tweed or velvet hats came in for sports wear in 1912. With the new smaller hats went a distinctive range of millinery mounts, all stiff and spiky where earlier they had been soft and draped. Aeroplane wings, hussar plumes, palm-effect ostrich feathers all made their appearance in 1911-12, while lancer plumes and 'Mephisto' feathers appeared in 1913.[8] Straw in colours of deep burnt orange, bright navy, grey and brown replaced the popular

Empire black. Turbans, reflecting the oriental influence conveyed through the Ballets Russes, were popular with evening dress.

In 1911-13 the hussar plumes were worn centrally on the helmet-shaped hats, the military effect curiously anticipating the coming crisis. When war broke out, Paris remained unoccupied and millinery was extremely lively, if chaotic, throughout the war years. The capital became an entertainment centre for soldiers on leave and the hat fashions set there could not have been more coquettish. The year 1914 saw an eighteenth-century revival with panniered skirts ending above the ankle and 'Watteau' hats. Cecil Beaton has described how 'Suffragettes tying themselves to the railings of Buckingham Palace now wore "Dolly Varden" shepherdess hats tipped up at the back with a bunch of ribbons under the rear of the brim'[9] (see figs. 41 & 42). Other styles were mannered and irregular variations on the tricorne shape, often projecting sharply to one side. In 1915 high postillion hats were worn while a year later 'Spanish' hats with wide straight brims were introduced and were always

---

41 Hat of Bangkok straw, claret colour, trimmed toning ostrich feather and gathered black velvet ribbon. Labelled 'Lambert Bernheim, Paris', 1914.

simply trimmed. Other wide-brimmed hats tended to form sharp points at the side when seen from the front. At the end of the war a distinctive shape of crown appeared which was to survive into the early years of the 1920s. This was a curious variation on the pork pie hat, giving rather the effect of a crust sharply risen to a point in a bowl with sloping sides.

42 *Advertisement in* The Tatler, *20 May 1914. The hat, top centre, is in the Bergère style and is similar to fig. 41.*

7

Women's Hats 1920 to the Present Day

The decade of the 1920s is popularly identified with a single hat style — the cloche. The helmet hats of the late 1920s, which were indeed adopted as a uniform, were the extreme point of a millinery fashion which had been evolving over a remarkably long period. We have seen how deep-crowned, bell-shaped hats first appeared in 1908 and how the depth over the brow and closeness of fit to the head became more pronounced in the years immediately before and after the Great War. It only remained for the 1920s to develop these tendencies to their utmost, and at the very end of the decade, to remove the brim altogether.

The first three years of the decade present an amorphous variety of styles. The distinctive crown shape noted in the last years of the war persisted, along with variations on the toque and tricorne forms. A large, plain picture hat, descended from the 'Spanish' hats of 1916, was popular for dressy wear. This style was trimmed in new ways. 'Glycerine' ostrich had appeared in 1919, the feathers treated to give a heavy, drooping effect which was repeated in the 'swagged' hats of 1922, with cascades of flowers

falling downwards towards the shoulder. Lace was also used as a falling curtain beneath brims. This downward fall in trimmings, reversing the shooting plumes of 1912 onwards, was a trend which would continue throughout the decade.

The 'bob', a longish pageboy style which had been introduced before the war by bohemians and trend-setters such as the dancer Irene Castle, became more widely accepted towards 1923. A year or so later, the 'shingle' introduced the new technique of razor cutting and by the mid-1920s, by means of cutting and Marcel, permanent or finger waving, the hair could be made to conform more closely to the shape of the skull. By 1924, a rounded, dome-shaped crown was definitely established in hats, and brims were pared away.

A felt hat in this form was essentially a 'hood' with the addition of minimal blocking and shaping. [1] The cloche proved an ideal fashion for mass-production and since it was worn by women of all ages and even by little girls, it created a boom for the felt hat industry centred in Luton. At the end of the war, manufacturers had imported hoods from abroad but from 1920 many found it worthwhile to produce their own. Felt was so well adapted to the cloche style that it virtually ousted all other materials from the Luton industry during the 1920s and early 1930s. Cloches for summer and the picture hats with narrow brims at the back and wide brims extending out to either side, which were the only alternative form to the cloche, were increasingly made from fibre straws of the continuously woven type such as baku, balibuntal and sisal. [2] These were manufactured, like felt hats, from hoods, and the traditional stitched straw plait industry went into a decline from

◁ 43 *Sports hat, the crown in alternate segments of white suede and suede printed in multicolour paisley patterns, c.1924. Leather hats in this style were popular for motoring while the fashion for printed suede can also be seen on shoes of the same date.*

which it never recoverd.

The years from 1926 to 30 were marked by attempts to 'streamline' the shape of the head. The 'Eton crop' of 1927-8 further revealed the outline of the skull and Brilliantine was used by women as well as men to give a sleek and shiny finish to the hair. Straws such as baku were varnished to further the likeness of the cloche to a metal helmet, since in 1926 the brim had been pared away almost completely. Already in 1923 Aldous Huxley had described his heroine as wearing 'a small sleek black hat that looked as if it were made of metal'. [3] In 1927 the rubber skull cap was introduced for bathing. There is a parallel with the fascination of Cubists such as Lèger with smooth, machine-made shapes and the sleek, seal-like sculptures of Brancusi. For the first time, the shape of a woman's skull was an important part of her appeal.

This new interest in revealing the shape of the skull required milliners to develop new techniques. One solution reached by the couture milliners,

44   Black felt cloche with brim dipping over one ear and attached scarf of black cashmere. Labelled 'Agnès, 6, Rue St. Florentin, Paris', 1929-30. The intricate seaming on model hats of the late 1920s — here, elaborate chevron patterns — is undetectable except at very close inspection. This hat was worn by the Ranee of Pudakota.

notably Caroline Reboux and Agnes, was to take the (custom-made) felt hood and fold the material at the side of the head into intricate shapes, rather in the manner of paper folding or Origami. The fluting of the brim which resulted was accepted as part of this sophisticated 'improvised' look. Slightly later, in 1928-32 the felt was intricately pieced and sewn together in a way that exactly corresponded with the jigsaw seaming carried out on the bias-cut dresses which were an innovation in dressmaking at this time. These two techniques were both typical of the under-stated chic which was the aim of the very rich. A similar result was achieved for the popular market by moulding the felt by machine into decorative ridges.

Such an uncompromising style as the 'helmet' cloche obviously did not admit of much surface decoration. Trimmings were chiefly confined to one side and were arranged with the 'downward fall' established at the opening of the decade. A brush-shaped arrangement of feathers was attached over one ear pointing downwards (see fig. 45) or, for a more informal effect, a scarf was tied around with pointed ends falling on the shoulder. When brims were pared away severely around 1926 the plain but intricate felt hats of society women were decorated with a single clip of precious stones — part of the craze for wearing gemstones, especially diamonds, with every outfit. Mrs Beste-Chetwynde in Evelyn Waugh's *Vile Bodies* (1928) wore 'a tight little black hat, pinned with platinum and diamonds'. Cheaper hats featured bakelite scarabs or embroidered or appliquéd motifs in the form of a badge.[4] Also on less severely chic models, various arty-crafty techniques were tried: ribbon work embroidery was popular and summer straws could be embroidered in raffia or painted.[5]

◁ 45   *Deep pink felt cloche with toning velvet hat band, piping and brush osprey. Labelled 'Maison Ross, 19 & 20, Grafton Street, London', c.1925. This style, with turned back brim and brush osprey on one side, is often seen in contemporary advertisements.*

46   *Hats from Barker's,* ▷ *Kensington High Street, c.1932-4. A variety of styles for the popular market, all of them hugging the skull and frequently dipping over one eye.*

The cloche hat, so modern and streamlined, blinkered its wearers no less than the poke bonnet of the 1840s. It imposed a period stance, since it was absolutely necessary to lift the chin and peer imperiously down the nose. The style was also a demanding one since the wearer was deprived of the flattering frame of hair or lace which had previously been considered indispensable. Its acceptance was helped by the new social tolerance of eye and lip cosmetics which gave definition to the face. Lipstick and eyeshadow were now widely used for daytime wear, though the use of mascara was still limited to evening.

From 1928 the hair was allowed to grow at the nape of the neck or hairpieces were added. The 'coalheaver' hats of this year had a brim which similarly extended down the back of the neck. At the same time, the front brim was lifted off the face, exposing the hairline, either folded back over the ears in Dutch cap fashion or extended to dip over one ear. This new asymmetry followed the hemline of the close of the 20s. The new shallower styles were favoured for dressy outfits while slouched felts with brims, Garbo style, were worn with sports clothes. Another of Garbo's hats, also designed for her by Adrian, the shallow, side-tilted style with ostrich feather trim worn in *Romance* (1931) achieved tremendous popular success as the 'Eugénie' hat of 1932.[6] By 1933, this sideways tilt, always to the right of the head, had become so universal that Agatha Christie's detective, Hercule Poirot, could identify his suspect by the unusual circumstance of her wearing her hat tilted to the left.[7] The new desire was to break free of the confines of the cloche and expose the hair, but designers still sought to fit the skull as closely as possible. Every kind of small hat shape was tried, provided it had no features which would interrupt the outline of the head. Knitted 'sock' hats were introduced by Schiaparelli, berets were made popular by Marlene Dietrich, and 'Juliet' caps, introduced in 1931, remained a popular evening and bridal fashion throughout the decade. Uncompromising modernity was replaced as an ideal by neatness or 'nattiness'. Colours and trimmings were subdued and matching cravats or gloves enhanced this effect.

Around 1934 milliners began to explore two devices which had not been taken up for a decade: height of crown and width of brim. A Tyrolean style was tried as part of an infatuation with Austria which also inspired the dirndl and the peasant blouse. The Cossack style consisted of a tube-like Astrakhan cap which developed two years later into the 'pouch' hat, described by James Laver as 'a handbag set on the head at a sharp angle'.[8] The 'Florentine' hat was popular around 1935, the tall crown tapering towards the top and leaning slightly forwards, a shape which was to continue throughout the later 1930s. Wide-brimmed hats had continued to be worn for garden parties and dinner wear but straight-brimmed sailor hats became extremely fashionable for daytime wear by 1935. In 1934 examples of the 'coolie' style appeared, as revived in the 1950s.

Considerable variety had been introduced into the millinery repertoire by 1936 and hats entered an increasingly fantastic phase in the years leading up to the Second World War. This year saw the first Surrealist exhibition in London and the movement proved to be a fertile ground for the decorative arts and for millinery. Schiaparelli actually collaborated with Salvador Dali on some of her dress designs and her fantasies in hats included the shoe hat of 1935, the lamb cutlet hat, the top hat of 1938, hats like baskets of fruit, and many others. A broader influence of the movement was felt in the increasing 'madness' of hats — 'The madder the hat, the smarter it is' pronounced *Vogue* in 1935.

Whereas the years prior to the First World War show the influence of light drama on fashion, those before the Second World War reveal the influence of the cinema. The effect of the Hollywood film costume designers was evident in these years chiefly by the heightened glamour of evening wear and the increased drama and fantasy in hats. Hats lent themselves easily to the cult of personality centring on the Hollywood stars. Film magazines ran regular features on the star's choice of hat styles and ordinary women were emboldened to adopt a consciously individualistic approach in their headgear (see Chapter 10). One specific example of cinema influence was in the Victorian revival of these years. A spate of costume dramas set in' this period throughout the 30s culminated in the phenomenal success of *Gone with the Wind* in 1939. The Eugénie hat was an early example, followed by forward-tilted hats in 1935. Unlike their prototype of the 1870s these hats were not secured by ribbons but were mounted at the correct angle on a close-fitting skull cap. Artificial flowers and veiling began to be lavishly used and dinner hats were adorned with feathers (see plate 8). A crocheted snood of 1860s derivation was introduced by Schiaparelli in 1935 and came into its own in the early years of the war as a practical device for keeping the hair tidy.

When war broke out, millinery fared very differently in England, France and the United States. In England hats were not rationed and so were available

◁ 47a New Hats for Autumn & Winter 1939 *(trade catalogue). Top, black felt Florentine style hat with hat pin in the form of a parrot and spotted veil. Bottom, Austrian style sports hat in mustard-coloured felt. Both examples of the popular high-crowned hats of the second half of the 1930s.*

47b *Dramatic feather trimmings were revived at the end of the 1930s.*
▽

as an antidote to Utility clothing. However, while the civilian population was subjected to air raids, this encouragement was countered by a trend towards going hatless or wearing severely practical headgear such as scarves tied turban-wise, hoods and knitted caps. In Paris, the fantastic tendency of pre-war millinery was whipped up to a frenzy in a spirit of defiance against the German army of occupation. The improvised turban of scarves was developed into an art form with endless variations, always of great height. All ingenuity was devoted to the design of hats which contrasted strangely with short, boxy skirts and wooden-soled shoes. Here and in the

United States of America where designers like Lilly Daché and John Frederics came into their own in the war years, styles were produced which were to reappear in post-war fashion.

The New Look, launched by Christian Dior in 1947 and influencing fashions during the first half of the 50s, was a conscious revival of the formal spirit of the couture before the First World War. As such, accessories like hats and gloves had an important role to play and were carefully considered by designers as part of the 'total look'. Hats were either very large or very small. The former included wide picture hats

which had evolved from the specifically mock Edwardian styles of the late 1940s decorated with winged feathers and motor veils; pointed crown 'coolie' hats and mushroom shapes. The smaller styles included pillboxes, boaters and a variety of small brimmed or brimless 'bonnets', worn on the back of the head exposing the forehead. After 1953 these sometimes featured points over the hairline, or widow's peaks. The bonnet hat evolved into the bandeau hat, like a saddle over the crown of the head and mounted on a flexible headband, which was a popular success of the mid-1950s. At this time, a Spanish influence reflected the status of Balenciaga as a couturier, and flat matador hats appeared, in moulded felt. In the late 50s a variety of cloche styles developed even deeper crowns and became the 'bucket hats' of 1958-9, with deep, down-turning brims, in tune with turn-down collars and bell-shaped skirts.

48   Three hats worn by Margot Fonteyn. Left, Mandarin style hat in black felt, by Aage Thaarup, mid-1940s. Centre, dark grey felt by Christian Dior, early 1950s. Right, black/pink shot velvet with black and pink osprey feathers, by Madame Vernier, early 1950s. The collection of hats worn by Margot Fonteyn, along with other collections of hats worn by one woman, all in the Museum of Costume in Bath, enable us to study the important role played by individual taste and personality in the creation of hats.

49 *Another group of hats all worn by one woman, a Mrs Hill of Denton Park, Yorkshire. Left, black velvet and fur felt by Renée Pavy, Mayfair, 1957-8. Top centre, grey feathers over pink silk tulle, labelled 'Charles Batten for Renee Pavy', c.1948-50. Bottom centre, brown velvet covered iridescent sequins, labelled 'Erik de Paris', 1952-4.*

The end of the 1950s and first half of the 60s were dominated by new trends in hairdressing. From 1957 hair could be set on rollers to produce fuller styles and backcombing (a new name for the teasing employed by the Edwardians) was widely used at the end of the decade to produce bouffant or bubble styles which echoed the short bouncy line in skirts. Hairdressers like 'Teasy-Weasy' Raymond in England and Kenneth in the United States became celebrities and after 1962 nylon wigs became popular as the ultimate in springy, resilient curls.

As this trend increased, milliners retaliated in four different ways. The first response was imitation. Hairiness was sought as an effect and shaggy, brushed mock beaver material was used for the cloche shapes of the later 1950s. Monkey fur was used in 1960 and fur hats of all kinds became popular, especially vast domes of shaggy fur. Also in the early 1960s, 'puffball' hats of ruched nylon net completely concealed the hair while they simulated its bouffant appearance, and similar hats of looped paper braid resembled pompom dahlias. These hats blurred the distinction between hat and wig, and contemporary magazines speak of the 'hatty wig'.

The second response was to make hats lighter, so that they would not spoil the result of hours spent in the hairdresser's salon. The milliner Paulette specialized in flower top knots on the flimsiest of net bases, and soft turbans of draped jersey.[9] Hats completely made up from artificial flowers were popular throughout the 1950s and 60s, and by the late 60s had

50 *Hat by David Shilling.*

become a byword as part of the uniform of middle-class ladies at a political or social gathering. Cocktail hats composed of only a gathered wisp of black nylon net, spotted or decorated with bows, enjoyed a similar popularity.

A few designers, notably the three Space Age couturiers, Cardin, Courrèges and Ungaro, deliberately sought to emphasize modernity in their hats. The former's high, domed helmet hats of 1959 got caught up with the hairdressing mania and were christened 'hairdryer hats'. Courrèges's 'baby bonnets' survived into the later 1960s in the form of large fur bonnets.

The final alternative was increasingly used in the late 1960s and during the 1970s. The 'youth revolution' of the close of the 1960s had jettisoned hats along with gloves, specific outfits for specific occasions and all the apparatus of genteel fashion which had been built up over one hundred years. By 1967, the 'big head' period of hairdressing was coming to an end and long hair, worn uncovered and unstructured into 'hairstyles' was a badge of liberation among young women. Designers tried to introduce styles for the younger market which would not frighten away customers with a dressy image. These were all utilitarian styles which did not require the traditional skills of the milliner. The masculine tweed cap was popular in 1961 after the success of the film *Jules et Jim* (and again in 1976); in 1963 Brigitte Bardot launched the headscarf, and headscarf-hats which were padded and stitched at the front became popular. That great staple of the 1950s, the pillbox, was made standard headgear for dressier occasions in the 60s by Jackie Kennedy. Large stetson, sombrero and Spanish riding hat shapes were popular from 1967 and were espoused by younger members of the royal family. The pull-on, rib-knitted cap was also popular from the late 1960s and still survives today.

During the 1970s, the preoccupation with showing heads of healthy natural hair, skillfully cut and blow-dried, furthered the decline in hat wearing. Older women who had been brought up to wear hats were served by firms such as Kangol who produced deep crowned styles in brushed felt exactly in the mode of the late 1950s. There was simply no current idiom for the hat proper. The latter survived in this period in the hands of milliners like Freddie Fox and John Cavanagh, who created hats for the royal family and those who attended royal occasions such as garden parties and race meetings. These hats were hats of ceremony, worn also for the symbolic occasions of ordinary people's lives, such as weddings, Bar Mitzvahs and school prizegivings. In 1981, the hat of ceremony thrived as never before, thanks to the impetus provided by the royal wedding and the hats for the Princess of Wales created by John Boyd.

The later 1970s saw a revival of hats in a new form, exploiting their potential to be outrageous or self-consciously stylish, once freed from their association with conformity and everyday life. David Shilling is the best-known exponent of this form and the extrovert clients he attracts, such as the journalist Molly Parkin, are not afraid of the impact of wearing a dramatic hat when all around go bare-headed. As an extreme instance of this trend, his clients say they leave their hats on display in their rooms when not wearing them, in the manner of objects d'art. [10]

Attempts made by the fashion trade and the press to launch hats for the popular market, such as the veiled 40s-style pillbox hats of 1979, have largely failed, since potential customers are caught in a vicious cycle of waiting for the fashion to establish itself before they try it. The majority of women, who have no wish to be conspicuous, are precluded from both of the present-day categories of hat wearing, the hat of ceremony and the hat of style.

8

Men's Hats 1900 to the Present Day

It is remarkable that the twentieth century, which has seen such dramatic changes in men's way of life, has produced no new style of hat which enjoyed any lasting popularity. All the types continued from the previous century, changing their roles subtly, while after the Second World War, headgear of every kind fought a losing battle against the rising tide of hat-lessness. The symbolism of men's hats in this century has tended to proclaim political rather than class allegiance.

Before the Great War, the wearing of some sort of hat was considered as much of a necessity as it had been in Victorian times. The silk top hat continued to accompany the frock coat and morning coat, and a gibus was carried with evening dress. The two types of formal daytime coat were, however, being gradually superseded by the lounge suit, and the top hat was therefore less often seen in the streets. Lamenting its decline, the *Hatters' Gazette* in 1903 protested that 'the frock coat and tall hat are absolutely essential as a foil to the elegantly gowned woman'. The homburg, trilby and bowler were all worn with the lounge suit. Brown was introduced as a popular colour for the latter from the United States where 'the brown derby' was the badge of a political movement.[1] For summer wear with the lounge suit, the boater was popular as never before, made from the light Japanese and Chinese straws which were imported in vast quantities. Its use was extended into the early days of winter, when it was sometimes made in brown or black. Paper versions were manufactured in Lyons in 1903, and later in Luton, though they did not enjoy the same success as the contemporary vogue for paper hats amongst women. Perhaps as a reaction to the enormous popular success of the boater, panama hats were increasingly worn by the Edwardian upper-class gentleman. They were inherently expensive: King Edward VII possessed one which cost 75 guineas.[2] The distinctive mark of the panama hat was the moulded ridge running from front to back over the crown. Stitched-brim linen sports hats were introduced around 1912 when a similar hat appeared

51 'Bank Holiday', by William Strang, 1912. The young man taking his girlfriend out to tea wears a light-coloured bowler hat with ribbon bound brim. The bowler was the 'best' hat for the less well off throughout the 1880-1914 period.

52 A crowd in front of Luton Town Hall, summer ▷ 1911. The boater was an enormous popular success for men and women of all classes from 1895 to 1914. Here it is seen on its home ground (the chief centre of manufacture was at St Alban's).

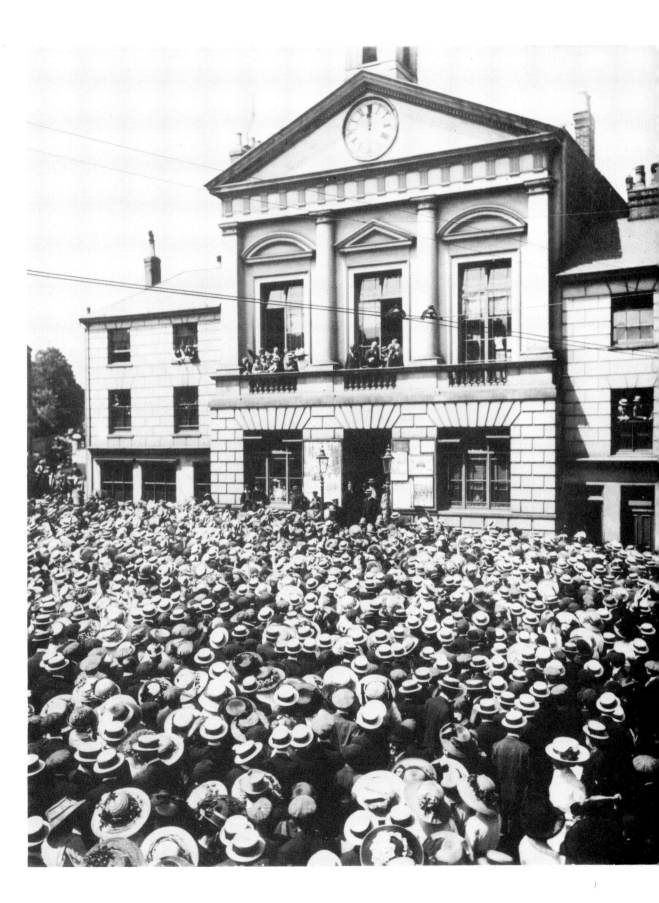

Town hats are lighter

Sports hats are weather-proof

Homburg hats 21/- 25/- 30/-

Light weight Sports hat (under 2oz) showerproof 17/6 Other qualities slightly heavier 21/- 27/6

Tweed Fishing hat 14/6

Tweed caps 7/6 10/6 12/6

Silk hats 35/- 42/- 50/- 55/-

Soft hats 21/- 25/- 30/-

Rough finished pork pie 12/6 21/- 25/-

Bowler hats 21/- 25/- 30/-

for women, and had some following, especially in the United States. The tweed cap enjoyed a popularity comparable with that of the boater, but its success was bemoaned by the trade journals since it was manufactured by small London firms rather than by the traditional hatting industry centred on Manchester and Luton. The Labour MP Keir Hardie wore a cloth cap on every public appearance and helped to identify it not just with the working man but with the Labour movement.

Just after the Great War a new form of trilby was introduced to meet the demand for a lighter, more comfortable and less easily crushed hat, to suit the faster pace of men's lives. This was known by the trade as a 'snap-brim felt' and was made of a very flexible felt which could be turned up at the back and down at the front. This hat virtually became a uniform for the city worker between the two wars. In the 1920s the fashionable form had a tall, pointed

◁ 53 *Portrait of the Prince of Wales by John St Helier Lander, c.1922. The Prince is shown wearing two of the fashions he helped to make popular, the knitted Fairisle sweater and the tweed cap with full, pancake crown, both popular wear with 'plus-four' trousers.*

54 *Advertisment for hats by Simpson's of Piccadilly, 1938. Lighter felts and methods of construction of hats were pursued by manufacturers, anxious to prevent 20th-century man from casting off headgear as being too formal and restricting. The two outstanding popular successes of this century, the boater and the snap-brim felt, were both essentially lightweight hats.*

crown and very wide brim, both features exaggerated in the outfit of the American gangster. The popularity of the trilby weakened the tenuous hold of other forms of hat. The top hat was worn on very formal occasions and was beloved of heads of state. The bowler took on the role of the 'posh' hat for the average man — Charlie Chaplin caricatured its pretensions in his films. During the 1920s and 30s the Americans were more inventive than the British with resort and sports headgear. Palm straw 'planter' hats with draped 'puggaree' bands of printed fabric were worn for the former and navy felt 'Basque' berets for the latter. In England, the Prince of Wales inherited the trend-setting role of his grandfather, and men copied him in wearing a full-crowned version of the tweed cap to accompany plus-fours.

55 Black felt homburg hat, labelled 'James Howell & Co. Ltd., Cardiff'. Worn by a clergyman in the later 1930s. The contemporary display head was made for the leading hat manufacturers of the late 19th and 20th centuries, T. W. Christy & Co. Ltd.

In a direct parallel with the earlier Prince of Wales, he made popular a Tyrolean style of hat in green with feather trim. During the 1930s, an informal variation on the trilby with a pork pie crown, seen earlier in the century in the United States, became popular wear with tweeds. The elegant Sir Anthony Eden as Foreign Secretary revived a tall-crowned black felt version of the homburg (see fig. 55). There was also a limited revival of the boater, as worn by Maurice Chevalier. The tendency to go hatless, promoted by the sun-bathing craze at the south of France resorts in the late 1920s and early 1930s, was furthered by the healthy life, open-air and hiking movements of the 1930s.

During the Second World War, supplies of hatter's plush from Germany were curtailed and trade was not resumed with the return of peace. The Associated

British Hat Manufacturers deliberately set out to substitute for the black silk hat the grey felt topper, used from the later nineteenth century for Ascot week only. With the co-operation of the press and leading personalities it was successfully established as the correct wear for royal garden parties and for weddings in the 1950s, and has survived for these occasions until today, reaching a wider public through the hire services of firms such as Moss Brothers. A similar wartime shortage of shellac threatened the existence of the bowler, but it was re-established and even revived after the war. The Duke of Edinburgh wore a bowler in 1949[3] and they were made regulation 'mufti' for Guards Officers. The Edwardian revival which affected men's tailoring in the early 1950s helped the acceptance of the bowler and the grey topper. However, the general trend was to wear hats less and less, even in the face of the effective slogan coined for the Associated British Hat Manufacturers, 'If you want to get ahead, get a hat'. In a further attempt to encourage hat wearing, the trade launched a new style of trilby in the second half of the 1950s, with a narrower brim and lower crown, sometimes made with a flat top, and worn with tapered, Italian-look suits. A version of this is still popular today among the racing fraternity. Flat tweed caps, also in a trimmer version, shorter from back to front, were worn with sports jackets and duffel coats. Fur hats in Cossack style were launched by Harold Macmillan after his 'Supermac' trip to Moscow, and had a limited following among commuters. Boaters disappeared altogether except as part of public school uniform, and panamas were worn only by elderly clergymen.

After 1965 the 'peacock revolution' in men's clothing introduced 1930s revival suits and with them gangster-style slouched felt trilbys, with very wide brims, sometimes made in coloured velour.[4] These hats were particularly espoused by those connected with the arts – Cecil Beaton, George Melly and Roy Strong among others, following in the long tradition which we have traced from the Elizabethan gallants through to the nineteenth-century bohemians. Black caps with short peaks were made popular by the Beatles. Both these 1960s styles were minority fashions, however, and many younger men at this time never wore a hat.

Today the top hat still survives for a limited number of formal occasions, but the bowler is rarely seen on the business man. Men's outfitters keep a small stock of tweed hats and caps for sporting wear and wooly pull-on skiing hats are worn in cold weather. The most colourful and original headgear to

be seen in big cities is sported by the immigrant community, the vivid turbans of the Sikhs and especially the monster knitted hats and inflated checked caps worn by West Indian supporters of the Rastafarian movement. These are occasionally joined by a second-hand trilby or other fancy dress hats which appeal to youth cults such as the New Romantics of 1981.

56 *Woman making boater hats, St Alban's, 1936. The boater enjoyed a limited revival in the second half of the 1930s.*

9

Caps for Men and Women

MEN

Caps were worn by men for informal indoor wear from the sixteenth to the end of the nineteenth century. During this long period they remained remarkably consistent as a type, in their function and even in their shape. Usually worn with a loose gown, they were referred to during the first three centuries of their existence as 'night caps' but should not be confused with the plain linen or knitted caps actually worn in bed. (The cloth caps worn outdoors for sport in the nineteenth and twentieth centuries have been

included in the chapters on men's hats.)

The form of the night cap in its first appearance in the sixteenth century continued throughout the seventeenth, being a deep round crown made in four conical sections with the border turned up to form a close brim. It was made either in silk, velvet or wool, but the majority of examples which survive from the

---

57 Men's night caps, early 17th century. Linen with embroidery in coloured silks and gold thread.

58 'Lord George Graham in his Cabin', by William Hogarth, c.1745. Lord George enjoys his pipe while wearing a night cap in turban style.

early seventeenth century are of linen, finely embroidered and quilted. A curious variation appeared at the beginning of the eighteenth century, in tune with the bizarre patterns of contemporary silks, whereby the crown was left open and folded into four corners which were tacked together where the points met at the centre and surmounted by a triangular funnel of fabric. After 1730, the nightcap took on a more specifically Eastern, turban-like appearance, made with a full-gathered crown and adorned with a tassel. The nightcap seems to have barely survived into the early years of the nineteenth century, but during the 1850s it underwent a transformation and gained a new lease of life as a 'smoking cap'. The form it took was a cross between the fashionable pillbox and the Turkish fez, and may owe some of its inspiration to the Crimean War. The smoking cap was once again made the vehicle for every kind of domestic embroidery, patchwork, silkwork and especially the crazes inspired by the East, such as applied Russian braid in

scrolling arabesque patterns, with elaborate macramé tassels and, after 1870, 'bandanna' embroidery on Indian printed scarves (see plate 6).

During the sixteenth and first half of the seventeenth century, night caps seem to have been particularly favoured by the elderly, but after the introduction of wigs they were more widely popular, as they afforded protection to the shaved head. When natural hair was once more fashionable in the early nineteenth century, informal caps were less seen, [1] but the social acceptance of smoking after the mid-nineteenth century extended their use once again. At all periods they were especially worn by artists and scholars who needed to work at home in conditions of warmth and comfort. They often chose to have their portraits painted attired in gown and cap as a badge of their calling. This genre of portraiture runs from the time of the architect Lord Burlington in the 1720s to the writer Thomas Carlyle in the 1860s. [2]

The average man of fashion donned his night cap immediately on rising in the morning and perhaps again at night, in the privacy of his own rooms. During the late seventeenth and eighteenth centuries, it was fashionable to receive close friends when wearing nightgown and cap, as a mark of intimacy and informality. It proved tempting to extend this morning period of ease. In 1711 Steele referred to men in coffee houses who 'come in their nightgowns to saunter away their time'. The same loungers probably wore caps and the same temptations were obviously felt in the spas: in 1742 the Rules for Behaviour laid down by Beau Nash, Master of Ceremonies at Bath, states that 'Gentlemen of Fashion never appearing in a morning before ladies in gowns and caps show breeding and respect'.

Another constant feature of the informal cap was its popularity as a present made by women for men. The Metropolitan Museum, New York, has a dated cap of 1566 made by Margaret of Parma for her Chief Counsellor, and in 1709 in the *Tatler* Old Isaac Bickerstaff described how his courtship of Miss Molly 'went so far that my mistress presented me with a wrought nightcap and laced band of her own working'. Similarly the majority of smoking caps in museum collections were made from patterns in ladies' magazines by wives and daughters for the paterfamilias.

The appeal of the informal cap is not difficult to understand. The eighteenth-century gentleman at ease in night cap and banyan no doubt indulged the fantasy of being a pasha returned from the East Indies, while for the Victorian male the attraction was heightened by the contrast between the colourful fantasy of his informal headgear and the sombre outfit of his public life.

WOMEN

Women's indoor headgear, although showing considerably more variety of form than men's, is similarly consistent in its definition and scope. Female caps inherited something of the role of the mediaeval veil: worn mainly indoors, made of linen or lingerie materials, designed largely to conceal the hair and considered especially suitable for the married woman and the bourgeois. Caps became associated with sobriety or domestic intimacy and were most widely worn when these qualities were in the fashionable ascendant, as at the end of the seventeenth and beginning of the eighteenth century, and in the early Victorian period. They finally disappeared in the 1890s, with the emergence of the more active ideal of the 'New Woman'. Morning caps, worn immediately after rising, tended to be less elaborate than the afternoon versions, while at various dates caps were fashionable for evening and even court wear. Night caps, worn for sleeping, were simplified forms of the current style in day caps and will not be described in detail here.

The actual form of the woman's indoor cap derived from the coif or close-fitting linen bonnet worn by men from the late twelfth century onwards. The coif was adopted by women in the sixteenth century and its form was basic to all later variations of the indoor cap. In the Jacobean period it was usually gathered with a drawstring at the neck and curved over the cheeks to reveal the side hair but conceal the ears. Specimens which survive are often finely embroidered like the contemporary men's caps, and some have a matching triangular 'forehead cloth' which is thought to have been an extra protection for the head during illness or at night. Coifs worn during the reign of Charles I often had a front band which was worn turned back like a cuff and decorated with lace and cutwork. Towards 1680 the sides were lengthened into long streamers or 'lappets' while the front was formed into several tiers arranged as upstanding pleats or flutes which required the support of a wire frame called a 'commode'. This extraordinary head-dress was christened a 'fontange' [3] and was extremely fashionable up to 1710. The lappets and flutes were frequently made of lace, since the encouragement given to the luxury trades by Louis XIV's financial minister, Colbert, had increased the manufacture and use of fine laces. The opportunity provided by the fontange for the lavish display of lace no doubt contributed to its fashionable prestige and it was worn on all occasions, indoors and out. Versions for court wear could be very costly, one in Brussels lace cost £40 in 1709. [4] Its dignity and formality accorded well with the more sober tone of the court of Louis XIV under the influence of Mme de Montespan and the court of the House of Orange and Stuart in England.

After 1712, the towering fontange became suddenly unfashionable. The *Spectator* of that year observed:

59 *Engraving after J. D. de St Jean, 1693. The tall,* ▷ *dignified lines of the 'fontange' cap echoed the long, stiff bodices and drawn back skirts of the end of the 17th century.*

'The ladies have been for some time in a kind of moulting season with regard to their heads, having cast great quantities of riband, lace and cambric'. The small round cap with lappets which had been the foundation of the fontange remained, but towards 1720, when the hair began to be dressed in a close knot on the summit of the head, the back of the cap was moved upwards to enclose it, revealing the upswept hair at the nape. The reverberations of the towering front piece were felt up to 1740, first in the form of small pleats of lace at the front and later as a single pinch at the centre forehead. The new smaller cap was known as a 'pinner' and two further variations appeared around 1730. The first, known as the 'round-eared cap', was worn on the top of the head like the pinner, but had a frill which did not extend round to the back, giving it a bonnet-like appearance. The round-eared cap could be worn at court, but the other new style, the 'mob cap', was essentially undress wear. It was distinguished by its puffed-out crown and deep, flat border, extending down the neck and ears. Caps were never more universally worn than during the reign of the first two Georges. They were worn by all classes and on all occasions, outdoors as well as indoors. This status is revealed by their contemporary name — they were referred to simply as 'heads'. Paintings by Hogarth between 1730 and 1750 depict women wearing caps to weddings (including the bride), the theatre and even in the tavern and brothel scenes from the *Rake's Progress.* [5]

During the 1750s when the side hair began to be dressed to stand out from the face, the frill of the round-eared cap was similarly starched or wired to

60 *'L'Atelier de Lingerea,' engraving from* Le Bon Genre, *c.1805. The girls are making 'lingerie bonnets' in corded linen, popular for morning walking wear throughout the first 30 years of the 19th century. Their own headwear shows popular styles of indoor cap.*

5 Bottom, bonnet trimmed with real twigs and artificial flowers, c.1884. Top, bonnet trimmed with imitation autumn leaves having a worm-eaten effect, 1887-8.

6 Group of men's smoking caps. Centre top, 'crazy' or irregular patchwork with appliqué animals in silk plush, 1880s. Left, dark blue velvet with applied silk braid, 1860s. Centre bottom, 'Anglo-Indian' embroidery, in chain stitch over printed cotton, 1870s. Right, wool cloth embroidered in floss silks, 1870s.

7 Leghorn hat, 1900-1904, labelled 'Gannaway, Broad & Strachan, Malvern'.

8 Group of feather-trimmed evening hats. Centre, black satin cap with ostrich feather by Caroline Reboux, c.1938. Left, suede cap trimmed with peacock feathers by Caroline Reboux, 1946. Right, 'coolie' style hat in satin and feathers, c.1936.

61 Left, morning cap, 1825-8. The high, puffed ▷
crown and wide frills repeat the lines of the contemporary bonnet, while the strings are similarly
left untied, as floating streamers.

fan outwards. In the 1760s this developed into forms
variously called the 'Pulteney', 'Queen of Scots' or
'butterfly cap', often in fine gauze or lace wired into
two rounded wings with a central depression. This
type of cap is usually depicted on older women, who
often added a lace or gauze scarf tied over the crown.
More informal styles were introduced for younger
women such as the 'Ranelagh mob', simply a square
of material folded diagonally, the ends crossed under
the chin headscarf fashion and tied at the nape of the
neck. This was copied from working women who
wore scarves tied over, or sometimes under, a hat or
cap. The turban also made its first appearance, being
a gauzy scarf twisted around the head.

During the 1770s and 1780s when hairstyles grew
to a fantastic size, caps tended to become similarly
large for undress wear while dress caps became very
tiny. The popular undress style of the 1770s was the
'dormeuse' which had a gathered crown loosely
enclosing the high toupée with pleated borders
curving over the cheeks 'like blinds to a horse's head
harness'.[6] Enormous mob caps were favoured with
the wide hairdressing of the 1780s. Dress caps were
improvised arrangements of puffs of tulle with long
floating ends while the turban became a scarf lightly
twisted around the toupée.

During the 1790s caps for daywear became less
fashionable while close-fitting silk caps and especially
turbans were worn with every type of half and full
dress toilette and were invariably trimmed with tall
nodding ostrich plumes. This situation continued into
the early 1800s with mob caps and 'biggins' (a cross
between the mob and the dormeuse) enjoying a
limited popularity for daywear, but every form of cap
and head-dress — including nets, handkerchiefs and
turbans — being worn with evening dress. The
'cornette' style was introduced around 1806, with a
tall conical crown rising to a peak at the back, and
became increasingly popular as the crown of hats
rose towards 1820.

As the brims of bonnets and hats expanded in the
later 1820s and early 1830s, the frills on day caps
were similarly gathered and starched to form an
aureole around the face. They were often trimmed as
elaborately as the outdoor bonnet, with coloured
linings, lavish ribbons and artificial flowers added
even to the morning caps. Silk gauze and blond lace

62 Dress cap, c.1865. Black spotted net, cherry
red silk and velvet ribbon, blond lace, artificial
flowers and pearls. The front is wired in the 'Marie
Stuart' shape. The dress cap, worn for dinner and
evening parties, enjoyed a revival in the 1860s.
▽

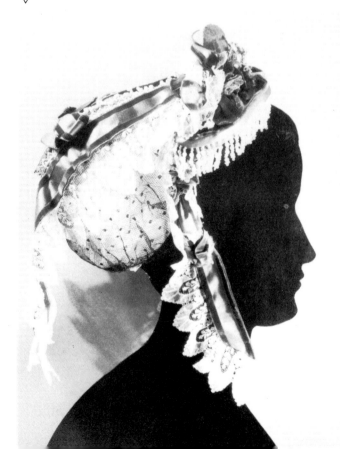

63 *Advertisement for boudoir caps, 1917. The boudoir cap, unlike its Victorian predecessor, the morning or indoor cap, employed many elaborate and unwashable trimmings, such as sequins, metal lace and fur.*

became popular for dress caps. Around 1833 a close-fitting style with a round, simple crown like a baby's bonnet was usual, but in the second half of the decade this was superseded by the 'babet' or 'paysan' cap with a high, puffed and gathered caul on the summit of the head. Evening caps increased in popularity in the later 1830s, after the collapse of the dramatic dress hats and berets of the Romantic period.

During the heyday of the bonnet in the late 1830s and 1840s the day cap also enjoyed a universal sway. All types were worn well off the forehead, but had frills descending low on the cheeks covering the ears.

Trimmings in the form of loops or rosettes of ribbon were also concentrated in this region. Head coverings of any kind were less popular in the evening, but a 'fanchon' style was worn, consisting of a triangle of lace with lappets extending from the side points. The

64 Group of boudoir caps, 1920-25, Left, silk printed in greens and blues, trimmed machine lace. Centre, coffee-coloured machine lace with gathered and appliquéd ribbon trim. Right, lemon-coloured georgette with ecru lace and coral and gold ribbon.

special status of the indoor cap in the life of the middle-class lady at this time is clearly brought out in Elizabeth Gaskell's novel, *Cranford*.[7] To older ladies like Miss Matty and Miss Pole, who were obliged to practise 'elegant economy', a new cap combined the virtues of unassailable propriety with the filip to one's wardrobe provided for wealthier women by a new dress or bonnet. 'The expenditure on dress in Cranford was principally in that one article referred to [caps]. If the heads were buried in smart new caps the ladies were like ostriches and cared not what became of their bodies.' When an unexpected caller arrived, the ladies of Cranford rushed to change their caps.

The advent of the hat and the first stirrings of emancipation in the second half of the 50s weakened the hold of the indoor cap. They grew smaller and lighter for daywear and were rarely seen in the evening. However, in the 1860s the dress cap made a comeback, possibly due to its similarity to the light and dressy form of the fashionable bonnet (see fig. 62). The elaborate construction usually featured a gathered caul enclosing the low chignon and long lappets, and incorporated velvet ribbons, black lace, pearls and artificial flowers. The fanchon style reappeared, this time as a day cap.

The leading style of the 1870s was the 'Charlotte Corday' with a gathered oval caul worn high on the head and a close frill. This was at first worn with hanging lappets, but these were abandoned towards 1880. By the later 1870s caps had ceased to be everyday wear for younger women and were worn only for breakfast and with the fashionable tea gown. At the end of the decade, they had been abandoned entirely save by the elderly woman. The night cap had a similar fate. The elderly continued to wear tiny dress caps until the end of the century, and even up to the First World War. The flattery of lace, ribbons, diamanté pins and artificial flowers helped to mitigate the severity of the all-black uniform which was increasingly adopted by the middle aged and elderly in the later Victorian period.

Around 1908 the cap made a surprise final appearance under the name of 'boudoir' cap. This may originate from the oriental-style turbans introduced for evening wear at this date by Paul Poiret. The oriental flavour of the boudoir cap was conveyed through the use of gold lace, tissue ribbon, brightly printed silk and even fur. Towards the 1920s it developed a closer fit to the skull and the form was extinct by 1930. As their name suggests, boudoir caps were worn for lounging with kimono style negligés and later with pyjamas, rather than with ordinary indoor dress or even with night wear. They were redolent of the world of ottomans, screens and tasselled cushions, christened by Osbert Lancaster as 'Style Ballets Russes'.[8]

10

The Art of Millinery

Unlike many of the skills employed in the making of clothes and accessories, millinery is not a craft with traditional skills and a guild organization. It emerged only towards the end of the eighteenth century and flowered during the nineteenth and first half of the twentieth century. During this time, its finest productions achieved the status of a minor decorative art. Hats are less constrained by the need to fit the body than any other item of clothing and can be a vehicle of fantasy for their creators and of self-expression for their weavers.

The original meaning of the word 'milliner' was a purveyor of fancy goods such as straw hats, gloves and other fancy articles for which Milan was famous in the sixteenth and seventeenth centuries. Diderot's entry for 'Milliners' in his *Encyclopédie* of 1765 states 'It is only recently that these tradesmen have established themselves and bear this name, in fact since they left haberdashery and took over the fashion trade'. By the 1770s the milliner had ceased to be merely a supplier of trimmings and accessories to costume and had become an arbiter of fashion, actually making caps and trimming hats and devising the ornaments for dresses. Milliners became the leading influence on styles in pre and post Revolutionary France: one of their number, Rose Bertin, who opened her shop in 1773 became the close confidant of Marie Antoinette and they created her outfits together. The emergence of millinery as an element of decoration, frivolity and fantasy in costume is a French phenomenon but the hats themselves, which became from the late 1770s onwards the chief focus for these qualities, originated in England. This marriage continued during the nineteenth and twentieth centuries: most of the finest exponents of the art of millinery continued to be French, but many of the innovations, such as the reappearance of the hat in the 1850s, stemmed from England. The leading English milliner of the 1770s and 80s seems to have been a Mrs Beauvais, whose customers included Queen Charlotte, Mrs Thrale and Marchioness Grey. [1]

In the early years of the last century the occupation

65 *Two miniature bonnets made by apprentice milliners (with full-size bonnet, 1863-5, included to give an idea of scale). Left, horsehair bonnet in spoon shape, 1863-5. Approximately half-size scale. Right, Quaker bonnet, silk covered, mid-19th century. All 19th century apprentices were required to make miniature versions of their craft to improve their skills, and milliners were no exception. Aage Thaarup may have had these miniatures in mind when he made tiny hats during the Second World War as pledges to be exchanged for full-size versions.*

66 *Advertisement by Madame Tucker Widgery,*
early 1890s. An enormous variety of millinery
was available to customers by the late 19th century
and, with 'any combination' of colours and trimmings
an offer, matching the hats to the outfits would
have posed no problems.

of milliner was still a fluid one, most often combined with that of dressmaker or haberdasher. (Millinery is a very seasonal trade and not until this century did many milliners rely entirely on the sale of hats.) Bonnets were given makers' labels earlier than dresses and examples can be found from the late 1830s. [2] The names of milliners are also noted in the credits to magazine fashion plates, which reveal that they were invariably women. However, no milliner emerges as a personality at this date except a Mrs Bell of 3 Cleveland Road, London, who revealed a flair for publicity not seen again until the late 1930s. Married to John Bell, proprietor of the two leading magazines of the 1830s, *La Belle Assemblée* and the *World of Fashion*, she included publicity for her hats and other wares thinly disguised as editorial for the magazines. [3] The lingerie hats popular from 1800 to 1840 appear to have been made by the workrooms which also pro-

duced caps, underwear and other fine linen accessories, though many were probably made at home.

The first important name in the field of millinery appears at the same moment as that of the founder of haute couture, Charles Worth. Caroline Reboux was the first member of what the French call 'haute mode' — millinery carried on at the same level and catering for the same customers as haute couture. She is said to have been professionally discovered in 1865 by the Princess Metternich (who is also credited with introducing Worth to the Empress Eugénie) and by 1870 she was installed in the heart of fashionable Paris at 22 rue de la Paix, where she continued to work until her death in 1927 aged over 90. A sable hat made by Caroline Reboux for the Empress Eugénie in the late 1860s is preserved in the Beaton collection at the Victoria and Albert Museum.

By the second half of the nineteenth century hats were available at every level of the fashion market. Milliners like Tucker Widgery (from the 1880s at 88 Westbourne Grove and later, as Madame Tucker Widgery, at 99 New Bond Street) advertised regularly in the *Queen* and other magazines, offering services which seem astonishing to the modern shopper. Models were available in any colour, trimming would be carried out free and an illustrated list could be sent post-free to any part of the world. The rise of the

67 'The Hat Shop', by Henry Tonks, c.1905. This
painting depicts the spacious and leisurely environ-
ment then considered necessary for the important
business of choosing the right hat.

great department stores also extended opportunities
for milliners and Peter Robinson, Jay's and others
had extensive millinery departments. Following the
renaissance of the hat in the late 1850s, England
was acknowledged to be the finest exponent of the
sporting hat, in felt or straw, plainly trimmed and
worn for country and informal town wear. This was
the province not of the milliner but of the 'ladies'
hatter', such as Henry Heath of Oxford Street, Mrs
White of Jermyn Street and Woodrow's of Piccadilly.

Lydia Bennet in Jane Austen's *Pride and Prejudice*
announces of her newly purchased bonnet, 'I shall
pull it to pieces as soon as I get home to see if I can
make it up any better'. Many women did not stop
short at this, but trimmed the entire hat themselves
from scratch and millinery became a popular hobby,
providing an outlet for artistic expression but re-
quiring less technical skill and equipment than dressmaking. Straw hats and bonnets were particularly

suitable subjects for the amateur, since until 1880
they were more simply trimmed than fabric ones
and when made of fine straws such as leghorn, were
frequently left unlined in the brim. Untrimmed
straws could be purchased from the warehouses (not
places for industrial storage in the modern sense, but
large retail emporiums devoted to one type of mer-
chandise). Some of these, like Meredith's Tuscan
Straw and Chip Hat Warehouse at Nottingham in the
1830s also advertised 'Hats Clean'd, Dy'd and Altered
to the newest Shape'.[4] From the 1870s fabric-
covered hats were made on 'foundations' or skeletons
of millinery wire covered in net and these too could
be purchased. (The wire foundation was not superseded until the 1930s when a coarse canvas known
as 'Spartre' was introduced.) To complete the creation
an extraordinarily wide range of ribbons and artificial
flowers was obtainable from the haberdashers and
feathers came from the stores or the specialist dealers
who were known as 'plumassiers'. After the late 1880s
magazines like *Weldon's Practical Milliner* were
available to give advice to the amateur.

During the late Edwardian period hats were ranked
so highly as a status symbol that many Society
women were tempted to set up as retail milliners. Mrs

68 Bill sent from Caroline Reboux to the Ranee of Pudakota. The Ranee ordered two hats for April, three for May and three for June. Another bill, from the same collection at Bath, reveals that she ordered 20 hats between May and December 1927. She also patronized other milliners, such as Agnès, Boucheron of London and Limard Soeurs of Cannes.

69 Letter sent by Suzanne, milliner at Caroline Reboux, to the Ranee of Pudakota, 28 October 1924. Suzanne encloses sketches and swatches of material, and asks for an accurate head measurement in case the Ranee's chignon is bigger − an important consideration for the skull-fitting cloches of this period. The purchase of a hat from one of the milliners of the 'haute mode' involved almost as much correspondence and as many fittings as a dress from the haute couture.

Peel who made this experiment around 1908 has recorded the perils involved in catering, as one of their number,[5] to Society women spoiled by practice of giving long credit, and conscious of the prestige value of their custom to the trader — not for nothing did shrewd milliners such as Tucker Widgery require 'trade references' in advance from customers. The hats and bills belonging to Heather Firbank, sister of the novelist Ronald Firbank, are preserved in the Victoria and Albert Museum and are evidence of the appetite for hat buying among the very wealthy at this time. One bill reveals that in 1909, at the height of the millinery season, from March to August, she bought twelve different examples of one type of hat, the popular boater, from Woodrow's of Piccadilly.

The creation of something as personal as a hat must always have required close collaboration between milliner and client, but this relationship is not recorded in detail until the 1920s. Many hats and some of the correspondence between the wealthy European wife of the Rajah of Pudakota and the firm of Caroline Reboux are preserved in the Costume Museum in Bath. A letter from her vendeuse at Reboux in 1924 encloses sketches of hats for consideration and requests an up-to-date head measurement 'in case your chignon is thicker than on your last visit' (see fig. 69). (The Ranee had evidently not succumbed to the bob.) Hats of the 'haute mode' would be made to measure and fitted as painstakingly as a dress or suit. It is astonishing that Caroline Reboux was still acknowledged to be the leading milliner to the smart international set of the 1920s, sixty years after the firm was founded.

Having discarded the modernist uniform provided by the cloche, millinery in the 1930s pursued a consciously individualistic role. Hats were used to emphasize and even exaggerate the personal characteristics of the wearer in much the same way as make-up and publicity created an image for the Hollywood stars. This lively trend encouraged a whole new generation of milliners, including for the first time some male recruits to the profession: in England, Aage Thaarup, Otto Lucas and Madame Vernier; in France, Suzy, Maud Roser and Paulette; in America the team of John-Frederics, Sally Victor and Lilly Daché. These milliners were responsible for the diversity of hat styles which is a noticeable feature of the later 1930s and were skilled in the arts of publicity. Aage Thaarup had a special talent for this: during the war he hit upon the idea of selling miniature hats to soldiers on leave as pledges which wives and sweethearts could redeem for the hat of their choice. Some of the new breed of milliners also took to print, publishing their memoirs during or after the war.[6]

As in other aspects of culture, this self-consciousness turned out to be a portent of approaching decline. This was not apparent in the immediate post-war period, however, and millinery enjoyed an Indian summer during the 1950s. Milliners coped successfully with a new development in the couture: first Balenciaga in the 1930s, then Dior and others in the 50s, took over the design of hats as part of their new concept of the 'total look', rather than having them supplied, as previously, by the 'haute mode'. In England the skills of high-quality millinery survived in the lean years of the 60s and 70s, through the hands of milliners to the royal family — Simone Mirman and John Cavanagh and more recently Freddie Fox and John Boyd.

In the 1970s David Shilling succeeded through a mixture of talent and flair for publicity in making himself a household name at a time when millinery had been in the doldrums for over a decade. At the age of twelve he made an outrageous hat for his mother, Mrs Gertrude Shilling, to wear at Ascot, and subsequent hats made for her became a traditional part of the Ascot scene. He has proved that although millinery must accept a limited role in the fashion world today, it can still be a vital art.

11

The Craft of Hatting
and the Etiquette of the Hat

In contrast to the increasing madness of female millinery during the last two centuries, the traditional craft of the hatter appears very sane indeed. The staple of the trade, felt, is probably the oldest textile material. While there is, as yet, no archaeological proof, it seems likely that early peoples discovered the propensity of fibres to mat together when warm

70 *'The Mad Hatter', illustration by John Tenniel to Lewis Carroll's* Alice's Adventures in Wonderland, *1865. The Mad Hatter's Wellington style hat is out of date, to emphasize his absurdity, but the use of hats to carry an advertisement was a common practice at this date.*

△

71 *A pair of wooden hat screws or stretchers, early 19th century. Until the introduction of the oval hat block in 1817, hat crowns were made round and had to be adapted onto their owner's head by means of these stretchers. Hat guards worn in Worthing, 1900-1910. Left, cord with clips to attach to hat brim and lapel. Right, bone toggle to pass through lapel buttonhole, screw to attach to straw. Boaters, light and wide-brimmed, were not the ideal headgear for windy seaside weather, and precautions had to be taken against losing them. Hat brush, to smooth the nap of silk hats, 19th century.*

and damp, before they learnt how to spin and weave yarn.[1] Wool felt is widely used to this day by the nomadic people of the north and central Asian steppes, but the European hatting industry has been complicated by a preference for the lighter and stronger felt which can be made from beaver fur.

Beaver-felt hats were known in England in the fourteenth century – the merchant in Chaucer's *Canterbury Tales* wore 'upon his head a Flaundrish beaver hat'. Men's hats were imported from Holland and Spain until the fifteenth century, but the English trade was probably well established by 1604 when the Worshipful Company of Feltmakers was incorporated. The elaborate process of obtaining beaver fur was recorded in 1604 by a Dutch merchant, who wrote that European skins were first sent to Russia to be used as coat trimmings and then re-imported into Holland, since used furs felted more easily.[2] By this date, the beaver's European breeding grounds were exhausted and after the Hudson's Bay Company was

Brushing Pa's New Hat.

Edith. "Now, Tommy, you keep Turning slowly, till we've Done it all round."

set up in 1670, North America became the chief supplier of skins to the trade. The United States also emerged as an important manufacturer of hats and in 1731 a Hat Act was passed in England to prohibit export of hats from the colony.

In the eighteenth century beaver felt was still preferred for the highest quality hats but mixtures of beaver and wool or wool and rabbit fur were used for the cheaper products. *A General Description of All Trades*, published in 1747, describes the organization of the English hatting industry at this stage. The craft of feltmaker and hatter were mutually dependent. The former produced 'hoods' which were finished and styled by the latter and an apprentice hatter had to satisfy the requirements of the Company of Feltmakers before going on to qualify as a hatter. The process or 'mystery' which the apprentice had to master can be summarized briefly here. The coarse guard hairs were plucked from the beaver pelt which was then brushed with a solution of nitrate of mercury to raise the scales on the fur shafts so that they would lock together firmly, a process known as 'carotting' (if carried out in a poorly ventilated room, the

72 Punch cartoon, 1860s. The topper of silk hatter's plush needed frequent brushing to restore its silken lustre.

mercury fumes could damange the brain, hence the expression 'as mad as a hatter'). The fibres were then cut from the skin and taken to a special bench in a draught-free area of the workroom known as the 'hurdle', over which was suspended a hatter's bow, like an oversized violin bow seven feet long, strung with catgut. The fibres responded to the vibrations of the bow as controlled by the craftsman, by separating and spreading themselves evenly until they had formed into a thick but loosely structured mat of material known as a 'batt'. Several batts were then shaped into a cone, reduced by boiling and 'planked' (or rolled by the craftsman, wearing special leather mitts) until a hood of firm, dense felt had been formed. It was then dyed and stiffened with shellac. At this point the hood left the feltmaker and was sent to the hatter's for blocking into the desired shape for the current style, lining and finishing. The skilled journeymen who worked as hatters were famed for their independance of mind and strong political views — the hatter's trade union, along with that of the brushmaker's, is claimed to be the oldest in the country.[3]

The inherent conservatism of style in men's hats has resulted in hatters' shops being a uniquely long-lasting feature of the London scene. The most durable of all is Lock & Co., still trading at 6 St James's Street, where it was established in 1765 by James Lock. Since James was the archetypal industrious apprentice and married his master's daughter, the firm can be traced back further still, to the hatter's shop set up at another address in St James's Street in 1676 by Robert Davis, father of James Lock's master. Scott's of Bond Street, incorporated with Lock's in the 1960s, had a less consistent family history but could also be traced back to the mid-eighteenth century. Lock's are true hatters in the eighteenth-century sense, since they sold hats made on the premises. Their customers were chiefly aristocratic, but their records show that even the aristocracy, like Henry Vernon, bought only one hat a year, each spring, from 1756 to 1760.[4] Nevertheless they kept their customers from one generation to another and provided them with many services, including re-blocking and re-lining old hats (sometimes very old, since quality men's hats were made to last) and supplying livery hats for their servants. Their price for a 'fine hat' (beaver felt) remained constant throughout the eighteenth century at one guinea.

In 1797, John Heatherington, a hatter at Charing Cross, was described by *The Times* as appearing in the Strand in 'what he called a silk hat, a tall structure having a shiny lustre and calculated to frighten timid people'. Silk plush thus appeared at almost the same moment as the top hat, and though the two were to become inseparable in the later nineteenth century, it was slow to be accepted. The final depletion of supplies of American beaver in the mid-nineteenth century ushered in the reign of the silk hat. The shiny lustre of hatter's plush had to be maintained by regular brushing, while Frederick Willis has described how the sharp dressers of the Edwardian era used to call in at their hatters' daily to have their silk hats ironed.[5] Other technical developments were taking place in the hatter's craft in the first half of the nineteenth century. The scientific approach to fit which is a feature of men's tailoring in this century was also being applied to hats. From 1817 they were made on an oval block, whereas previously they had been made circular and shaped to the wearer's head by using a hat-screw. For the made-to-measure trade,

the 'conformateur' invented by M. Maillard in mid-century and shaped like a giant hat could be placed on the customer's head where it mapped its contours exactly, recording them precisely to scale on a card. Steam power was applied to the sorting of fibres in 1821 and the hatter's bow was replaced by steam blowing processes in the 1880s. These developments and the introduction of machine blocking paved the way for the hat manufacturers, industrial firms combining felt making and hatting, who established themselves in the north of England in the later nineteenth century, such as Battersby's of Stockport, and Christy & Co. The felt-making workshops in Southwark declined.

After the Great War, the concern of the hat manufacturers was to produce ever lighter felts in an attempt to overcome the modern man's increasing reluctance to wear a hat. Today the manufacture of fur-felt hats is carried on by a limited number of firms in the Manchester area, while a similarly specialized trade in wool-felt hats is concentrated on Atherstone in Warwickshire.

THE ETIQUETTE OF THE HAT

The etiquette of hat wearing for men hinges largely on the removal of the hat, for women on its retention.

The male gesture of removing the hat derives from its principal social function which is to confer status upon the wearer: taking off the hat in another's presence implies recognition of a superior authority. During the seventeenth century the hat could convey the exact degree of deference due to a superior, though this might require nice judgement especially where the royal family was concerned. In July 1663 Samuel Pepys passed the king's brother, the Duke of York while both men were strolling in St James's Park. Pepys removed his hat and remained uncovered until he was some distance away from the Duke but 'feared I might not go far enough with my hat off'. The Quakers alone would not acknowledge the social distinctions behind 'hat honour': their founder George Fox refused to take off his hat at Launceston Assizes before Cromwell's magistrates.

Seventeenth-century hats were worn for a much greater proportion of the day than in later centuries. They were always worn indoors, including at meal times and Pepys complained in 1664 that he had 'caught a cold by flinging off my hat at a dinner'. There is also some evidence that they were worn in church in this century. Pepys again commented that in church in 1661 he had 'heard a simple fellow exclaiming against men's wearing their hats on in the Church'.

By the eighteenth century the general adoption of wigs had subtly changed the manner of removing the hat in salutation. Previously, it had been lifted off and brought to rest against the thigh, crown outwards, but in the late seventeenth and during the eighteenth centuries the lining could be boldly displayed without fear that the owner would be shamed by its soiled condition. The practice was exploited in Pitt's Hat Tax of 1783 which required that a paper receipt be affixed to the lining of the hat to prove that tax had been paid — this was amended in 1796 in favour of a more durable stamp.

With the adoption of the neat and easily portable tricorne it became less important actually to wear a hat on all occasions and carrying one was considered a sufficient mark of good breeding. There is some evidence that this flexible attitude also applied to the correct etiquette in church. The *Connoisseur* of 1756 observed that, on entering a fashionable church, 'the beaux very gravely address themselves to the haberdasher's bills glewed to the linings of their hats'. However, it seems that they were sometimes put on again at sermon time to enable the wearer to snooze undetected: the Rules of Conduct for the Chapel Royal, St James's Palace, in the early eighteenth century stated that when royalty were present, 'no man shall presume to put on his hat at the sermon'.

Throughout the nineteenth century one gentleman would doff his hat to another if of higher social status or greater age, and always to a lady, and to her escort. The procedure when paying calls was described by Mrs Humphrey in 1897 in *Manners for Men*. The male visitor has taken off his coat when entering the hall but carries his hat upstairs; 'the hostess will probably say "would you not like to put down your hat?" indicating some spot where he may lay it. The reason of carrying the hat to the drawing room is a somewhat subtle one. It is based on the supposition that the masculine caller feels himself privileged in being permitted to pay his respects, and, feeling himself on sufferance is ready to leave at a moment, hat in hand, should he not find his presence agreeable and acceptable. I have a private theory that this custom is cherished and kept by men from a conviction that their hats are much safer in their sight ... than they would be downstairs in the hall.' It is amusing to note that men visiting the photographer's studio fell naturally into this drill and posed with their hats placed on the table beside them, so that the etiquette of the drawing room is faithfully reproduced in carte-de-visite photographs.

In 1903 the *Hatter's Gazette* lamented that the custom of taking off the hat as a sign of respect was 'fast falling into disuse as between gentlemen'. After the Second World War, the custom similarly declined in relation to women.

The etiquette of women's hats is based on the need to cover the hair for reasons of modesty and propriety. This was always strictly observed by the bourgeois wife in the seventeenth and eighteenth centuries, but aristocratic women of whatever marital status seem to have had no moral qualms about appearing bareheaded in public. The limiting of hats to informal wear in the mid-eighteenth century was based on a purely fashionable distinction. After the re-emergence of the hat in the mid-nineteenth century, the bonnet gradually took on the role of the 'proper' choice in headgear. It was particularly important for the nice-minded woman to wear a bonnet in church and ladies were very solicitous in seeing that their servants wore a bonnet for divine service, sometimes issuing them with one for the purpose. Ladies were expected to wear hats outdoors but also retained them indoors in circumstances where it would be difficult to remove them and still more difficult to put them on again with all the care and fine adjustment which this involved. Therefore ladies paying social visits would retain their hats while their hostess could always be distinguished by the fact that she wore an indoor cap or went bareheaded. The most controversial example of this kind of situation was in the theatre, particularly during the 1820s and 30s, and again in 1895-1910 when hats were not only very large but extremely fashionable and their owners were anxious to get a good audience for them. It was considered more seemly to wear a small hat such as a toque to matinées and to go bare-headed in the evening and don a gossamer scarf or 'fascinator' for the journey home.

The Victorian attitude to the wearing of all forms of headgear was grasped by Gwen Raverrat, writing of her childhood in the 1880s: 'Males and females alike, we had always to wear something on our heads out of doors. Even for children playing in the garden this was absolutely necessary. According to the weather we were told that we should catch a cold or get sunstroke if we went bareheaded. But the real reason was that it was proper — that the hat was an essential part of the dress.'

Notes

CHAPTER 1

1 See *Handbook of English Mediaeval Costume* by C. W. & P. Cunnington, p. 178, '. . . apprentices [in the fifteenth century] wore no headgear in their master's presence and the latter wore more important looking hats than their employer'.
2 See portrait of Prince Rupert of the Rhine by Gerard von Honthorst, c.1635, reproduced in P. Byrde *The Male Image*, p. 181.
3 Most noticeable in French engravings of this date, especially those of Jacques Callot.
4 Portrait of Charles I by A. Van Dyck, 1635, Louvre, Paris.
5 Philip Stubbes, *Anatomy of Abuses*, 1583.
6 See anonymous conversation piece in the Paul Mellon collection: English Cognoscenti in Rome, c.1750 reproduced on p. 147 of C. Hibbert *The Grand Tour*.
7 Lord Chesterfield, *Letters I*, pp. 249-50.
8 Portrait dated 1786 in Stadelisches Kunstinstitut Frankfurt, reproduced on p. 151 of C. Hibbert, *op. cit.*

CHAPTER 2

1 Thomas Platter, *Travels in England*, 1599.
2 'Callisto' or Court Masque of 1675 described in B. Baines, *Fashion Revivals*, p. 76.
3 R. Ryder, Diary 1715-16 (1939). Entry for 3 August 1716.
4 Thomas Coryate, *Crudities*, 1611, records that in Piedmont he saw 'most delicate strawen hats which both men and women use in most places of that province . . . some of them having at least an hundred seames made with silk'.
5 There were three main categories of dress in eighteenth century England: court dress, full dress and undress. See A. Buck, *Dress in 18th Century England*.
6 W. Moritz, *Journeys of a German in England*, 1782, quoted in A. Buck, 'Variations in English Women's Dress in the 18th century', *Folk Life* vol. 9, 1971.
7 H. F. Gravelot, 'An English Lady', engraved 1744-5, reproduced on p. 22 of M. Ginsburg, *An Introduction to Fashion Illustration*.
8 Portrait of Eleanor Francis Dixie by Henry Pickering (1750s). On display in the Museum of Costume, Nottingham.
9 Portrait of Nelly O'Brien by Sir Joshua Reynolds (1760-62), The Wallace Collection, London.
10 Examples of this type are in the collections of Luton, Nottingham, Worthing and Worcestershire County Museums.
11 Example in collection formerly on loan to Exeter Museum, see P. Inder, '18th Century Hats in Exeter Museums', *Costume* VII, 1873.
12 Example in Luton Museum.
13 Example in collection as (11).
14 Geoffrey Squire, *Dress, Art & Society* (Studio Vista).
15 'Morning Employment', 1785-8, engraved after H. W. Bunbury, reproduced in A. Buck, *Dress in 18th Century England*.
16 Hats of this type can be seen in 'The Haymakers' and 'The Reapers' (1785) by G. Stubbs in The Tate Gallery, London.
17 *The New Lady's Magazine*, 1787.
18 *The Ipswich Journal*, June 1799.

CHAPTER 3

1 Caricatures in *Le Bon Genre*, 1814 and 1815. This magazine talks of Englishwomen's 'little flat hats, long lank corsets and badly cut skirts'.
2 *Ackermann's Repository*, May 1815.
3 Depending on whether the strings were attached to the bonnet lining next to the face or to the very ends of the bonnet brim.

CHAPTER 4

1 The use of several primary colours within one

outfit was commented on by Hippolyte Taine in his *Notes on England* (1860).

2 Quoted from 'Ode on the Burial of the Spoon Bonnet'. *Punch*, 7 January, 1865.
3 Cartoon 'Pleasures of the Seaside' in *Punch*, 2 September 1865.
4 *Englishwoman's Domestic Magazine*, January 1879.
5 'Worm-eaten leaves' are quoted in Notes for 1879 in C. W. Cunnington, *Englishwomen's Clothing in the 19th century*. 'Faded Field Flowers', quoted in the *Queen*, August 1878.
6 *Woman's World*, 1889.
7 *Lark Rise to Candleford* (1945).
8 Example in the collection of the Victoria and Albert Museum.
9 Example in Gallery of English Costume, Platt Hall, Manchester.
10 Trade catalogue for 1901 in collection of Luton Museum.

CHAPTER 5

1 *The Hatter's Gazette*, 1878.
2 Portrait of the Prince of Wales, 1846, in collection of Her Majesty the Queen, reproduced in E. Ewing, *History of Children's Costume* (Batsford, 1977).
3 In collection of Her Majesty the Queen.
4 Reproduced in A. Gernsheim, *Fashion and Reality*.
5 See account in F. Whitbourn *Mr Lock of St James's Street*.
6 P. Cunnington and C. Lucas, *Occupational Costume in England*.
7 A. Gernsheim, *op. cit.*
8 After the hats depicted in George du Maurier's novel, *Trilby*, 1895.
9 G. & W. Grossmith, *Diary of a Nobody*, 1892.
10 Flora Thompson, *Lark Rise to Candleford*.

CHAPTER 6

1 *Weldon's Home Milliner*, 1900-1904.
2 Example in Worthing Museum. The average length at this date would be 10-12 inches.
3 C. W. Cunnington, *English Women's Clothing in the Present Century*.
4 Circles of stiffened fabric placed inside hat to fill out the gap between head and hat – the 'Fitzall' was a popular make.
5 Examples c.1905-8 in the Museum of London and the Costume Museum, Bath.
6 Acts banning the importation of rare plumage were passed in the United States of America in 1913 and England in 1921.

7 Roller skating, a craze in 1910 (and previously in the 1870s).
8 'Mephisto' feathers were a pair of long thin plumes curved into a hook at the end, as depicted in illustrations to *Faust*.
9 Cecil Beaton, *The Glass of Fashion*, Weidenfeld & Nicholson, 1954.

CHAPTER 7

1 The basic shape made by the feltmaker for blocking and finishing by the hatter – See Chapter 11.
2 Sisal was first introduced in 1926 and produces a linen-look weave.
3 *Antic Hay*, novel of 1923.
4 Felt hat with scarab brooch in collection of the Museum of London.
5 See M. J. Rendell 'Millinery Techniques in the 1920s' *Costume 12*, 1978.
6 For an account of the work of the film designers including Adrian, see *Hollywood Costume Design* by D. Chierichetti (Studio Vista).
7 *Lord Edgware Dies*, 1933.
8 *Taste and Fashion* by James Laver.
9 Some examples of her hats of the 1950s are in Nottingham Costume Museum.
10 *David Shilling: The Hats*, Ulster Museum, 1981.

CHAPTER 8

1 The Democratic Party and especially Alfred E. Smith, governor of New York.
2 *The Hatter's Gazette*, 1901.
3 To open the Ideal Home Exhibition, 1949.
4 Two hats of this style, made by Herbert Johnson, are in the Beaton collection at the Victoria and Albert Museum, one in scarlet and the other in olive-green brushed velour.

CHAPTER 9

1 A fashion plate of 1838 in *La Mode* shows a man wearing a tasselled cap with a dressing gown.
2 Portrait of Lord Burlington by J. Richardson, c.1720, National Portrait Gallery.
3 Named after Mlle de Fontanges, mistress of Louis XIV.
4 'The Postbag', 1709 quoted in C. W. and P. Cunnington, *A Handbook of English Costume in the 18th century*.
5 Weddings: 'The Wedding of Stephen Buckingham

to Mary Cox', c.1729 (Metropolitan Museum, New York).
Theatre: 'The Indian Emperor', 1731 (private collection). 'The Rake's Progress', 1735 (The Tate Gallery).
6 *The London Chronicle*, 1762, quoted in C. W. and P. Cunnington, *op. cit.*
7 Published 1853, drawing on the author's experience of the 1830s, but combining features of both dates.
8 Osbert Lancaster, *Homes Sweet Homes*.

CHAPTER 10

1 Anne Buck, *Dress in 18th Century England*.
2 A chip bonnet covered in pink silk, late 1830s, in the collection of The Gallery of English Costume, Manchester, is labelled 'Original Albion House/J. James, Maker/95 Oxford Street, London'. This probably refers to the

straw bonnet manufacturer: for an example of an early milliner's label see plate 3.
3 A. Adburgham, *Shops and Shopping*.
4 On a paper label inside a leghorn bonnet of c.1830-35, in Nottingham Costume Museum.
5 C. S. Peel, *Life's Enchanted Cup*.
6 For autobiographies by Aage Thaarup and Lilly Daché see Bibliography.

CHAPTER 11

1 The patron saint of hatters is St Clement, who is said to have put wool in his sandal to relieve blisters and at the end of his journey the motion of walking (pressure) plus perspiration (moisture) had produced a mat of felt.
2 Quoted in E. Ewing, *Fur in Dress*.
3 F. Willis, *A Book of London Yesterdays*.
4 F. Whitbourn, *Mr Lock of St James's Street*.
5 F. Willis, *op. cit.*

Bibliography

STUDIES OF HATS
H. Amplhett, *Hats: A History of Fashion in Head-wear*, Richard Sadler, 1974.
G. de Courtais, *Women's Head-dress and Hairstyles*, Batsford, 1973.
R. Turner Wilcox, *The Mode in Hats and Head-dress*, Scribners, New York, 1959.

BOOKS WITH SUBSTANTIAL REFERENCE TO HATS
B. Baines, *Fashion Revivals*, Batsford, 1981.
A. Buck, *Dress in 18th century England*, Batsford, 1979.
A. Buck, *Victorian Costume and Costume Accessories*, Herbert Jenkins, 1961.
P. Byrde, *The Male Image: Men's Fashion in England 1300-1970*, Batsford, 1979.
C. W. & P. Cunnington, *Handbook of English Costume in the Seventeenth Century*, Faber.
C. W. & P. Cunnington, *Handbook of English Costume in the Eighteenth Century*, Faber.
C. W. Cunnington, *English Women's Clothing in the 19th Century*, Faber, 1937.
C. W. Cunnington, *English Women's Clothing in the Present Century*, Faber, 1952.

E. Ewing, *Fur in Dress*, Batsford, 1981.
A. Gernsheim, *Fashion & Reality*, Faber, 1963.
J. Laver, *Taste and Fashion*, Harrap, 1945.

CONTEMPORARY JOURNALS
Fashion Magazines
For an account of these see: D. Langley Moore, *Fashion through Fashion Plates 1771-1970*, Ward Lock, 1971.
M. Ginsburg, *An Introduction to Fashion Illustration*, HMSO, 1980.

Trade Journals (all published in London)
The Hatter's Gazette, 31 January 1877-December 1958.
The Millinery Record, February 1896-June 1903, continued as *The Millinery and Mantle Record* until October 1903.
The Millinery Journal, April 1893-October 1897.
Millinery, February 1911-September 1912.
The Draper's and Milliner's Trade Journal continued as the *Drapery Journal* January-August 1922.

For the Amateur Milliner
Weldon's Practical Milliner 1880-1895.

Weldon's Home Milliner 1895-1928.

BIOGRAPHIES AND AUTOBIOGRAPHIES OF HATTERS
AND MILLINERS

Hatters
F. Whitbourn *Mr Lock of St James's Street*,
Heinemann, 1971.
F. Willis, *A Book of London Yesterdays*, Phoenix
House, 1960.

Milliners
Lilly Daché, *Talking through my Hats*, Cassell, 1956.
Aage Thaarup, *Heads and Tales*, John Gifford, 1946.
Hat Shops
A. Adburgham, *Shops and Shopping.*
C. S. (D.C.) Peel, *Life's Enchanted Cup*, 1933.

ARTICLES
All the following appeared in *Costume*, the Journal of
the Costume Society:

P. Clabburn, 'A Provincial Milliner's Shop in 1785',
No. 11, 1977.
P. Inder, '18th Century Hats in Exeter Museums',
No. 7, 1973.
T. J. Rendell, 'Millinery Techniques in the 1920s',
No. 12, 1978.
The following appeared in *Folk Life*, Journal of the
Folk Life Studies Group:
A. Buck, 'Variations on English Women's Dress in the
18th Century', vol. 9, 1971.
A. Buck, 'Dress as a Social Record', vol. 14, 1976.

MUSEUM PUBLICATIONS
C. Freeman, *Luton and the Hat Industry*, Luton
Museum, 1953, reprinted 1976.
M. Ginsburg, *Fashion: an Anthology by Cecil Beaton*,
HMSO, 1971.
E. McCrum, *David Shilling: the Hats*, Ulster Museum,
Belfast, 1981.

Glossary

Terms used in the text are listed here for easy reference. For a comprehensive dictionary of costume terms see *A Dictionary of English Costume 900-1900* by C. W. & P. E. Cunnington.

MEN

Bicorne nineteenth-century name for a style of hat worn 1770-1800; wide brims cocked at the front and back only, forming a half circle when seen from the front.

Bollinger 1840s-1860s' hat with bowl-shaped stiffened crown, often topped with a button or knob, and narrow brim. First worn by cab drivers and later by gentlemen for country wear. Also known as the 'hemi-spherical hat'.

Bowler 1860 onwards, hard felt hat with domed crown and narrow brim rolled up at sides. Name derives from William Bowler, feltmaker, who is said to have helped in making the prototype for the style. (*See also* Coke; Derby.)

Cambridge 1865-1900, a variation on the bowler hat with a flat-topped crown. Named after the Duke of Cambridge.

Castor seventeenth to nineteenth century, a hat made from beaver fur felt, from the Latin name for the animal (a 'demi-castor' indicated that a

mixture of wool or rabbit fur had been added to the beaver).

Chimney pot a mid-nineteenth century variation of the top hat with a very tall crown tapering slightly towards the top.

Coke nineteenth century, another name for a bowler hat, deriving from William Coke of Norfolk who is said to have devised the prototype for the style.

Copotain sixteenth and seventeenth centuries, a hat with a tall conical crown and moderate brim, especially fashionable from 1560 to 1620.

Cumberland 1830s' variation on the top hat with a tall, narrow crown tapering towards the top.

Derby nineteenth and twentieth centuries, the American name for a bowler hat, named from the popularity of that headgear at Epsom Races.

Fedora nineteenth and twentieth centuries, American name for a trilby hat, named after the play of that name by Victorien Sardou.

Gibus 1840 onwards, top hat with fabric crown which concealed a metal framework on the lazy tongs principle, enabling the hat to be collapsed for carrying under the arm. Named after the inventor.

Glengarry 1860s Scotch bonnet, higher in front than behind.

Homburg 1870s-1960, stiff felt hat with a dent running from front to back over crown, and a braided brim curved up at the sides. Made fashionable by the Prince of Wales who visited Homburg.

Kevenhuller 1740s-60s, large cocked hat with the front cock pinched into a sharp peak.

Monmouth cock second half of seventeenth century, manner of turning up hat brim sharply at back only.

Muller-cut-down 1864-1900, top hat with crown half the height usual at the period. Named after the murderer of that name whose wearing of the style led to his identification.

Night cap fifteenth to nineteenth century, two meanings. Either a plain washable cap worn for sleeping, or a skull cap with close brim made in fine materials or embroidered and worn informally indoors.

Nivernois 1760s' large three-cornered hat with the cocked sections rolled over a flat crown.

Opera hat second half of eighteenth century, flat three-cornered hat designed for carrying under the arm. Also known as 'chapeau bras'. 1800-1830, flat carrying hat made in bicorne form with stiff crescent-shaped brims and soft fabric crown.

Petasos Wide-brimmed hat worn by travellers in ancient Greece.

Slouched hat eighteenth and nineteenth centuries. Hat with a flopping or uncocked brim.

Smoking cap 1850-1900 indoor cap usually made in pork-pie shape, embroidered and trimmed with a tassel.

Stove pipe mid-nineteenth century top hat with a tall crown, the sides absolutely vertical.

Sugarloaf 1640-60 (also female) hat with tall crown as in copotain, but with wider brim.

Tricorn(e) nineteenth century name for three-cornered cocked hat worn during 1690-1800.

Trilby c.1870s – present day. Soft-framed felt hat with dent in crown. The name dates from 1895 after the novel of that name by George du Maurier.

Wellington 1820-40, top hat with crown wide at top and curving inwards towards brim.

Wideawake nineteenth century broad-brimmed low crowned felt hat for country and informal wear.

WOMEN

Babet 1836-50, cap with small puffed caul set high on the head, the sides descending over the cheeks. Also called paysan.

Balloon 1783-5, hat with an inflated gathered crown and a wide brim, usually made of a light fabric over a foundation. The name commemorates the pioneering balloon ascent of 1783. Also called lunardi or parachute.

Bergère 1730-1800 and again 1860s, straw hat with low crown and wide brim. Also called sheperdess or milkmaid.

Bibi 1831-6, bonnet in which the wide brim rears upwards, exposing the forehead but not the cheeks, and meets the high crown at an acute angle.

Biggin early nineteenth century, a large form of mob cap with a frill forming a curved edge and no ties.

Boudoir c.1908-30 a cap usually made of lingerie materials but with elaborate trim, worn with a negligee for lounging.

Capote 1800-1840 a bonnet with a soft fabric crown and a rigid brim in stiffened fabric or straw.

Caul eighteenth and nineteenth centuries' soft, pliable crown of a bonnet or cap.

Charlotte Corday c.1865-85, bonnet or cap with small puffed crown enclosed by a band and narrow frill, worn towards the back of the head. With or without lappets.

Cloche chiefly 1908-33, a hat shaped like an inverted bell.

Coalheaver c.1928-30, a cloche hat with no front brim and a flap hanging down at the back of the neck as in the hat worn by coal and dustmen at the time.

Coif sixteenth and seventeenth centuries a linen indoor cap with sides curving forwards over the ears. Often worn with a forehead cloth.

Coolie c.1934 and 1950-60 a round hat with pointed crown as worn by the Chinese.

Cornet(te) 1800-1840 indoor cap with a puffed and sometimes pointed crown, gathered into a broad band around the face which is continued under the chin.

Cottage bonnet early nineteenth century simple close-fitting straw bonnet, the sides projecting beyond the face.

Dolly Varden c.1871-5 a low-crowned straw hat with the sides bound around the head with ribbon and worn at an extreme forward tilt.

Dormeuse second half of eighteenth century, indoor cap with puffed crown, the pleated border exposing forehead, but wrapping cheeks and continued beneath chin.

Drawn bonnet 1820-70 composed of fabric gathered onto canes, whalebones, wires or cords.

Empire bonnet 1865-70 small close-fitting bonnet like a baby's cap exposing the forehead and back neck.

Eugénie 1932-5 small skull-fitting hat with rolled

brim worn to one side of the head and trimmed with ostrich plumes. Based on a hat worn by Greta Garbo in the film *Romance* (1931).

Fanchon　1840s a cap; 1860s a bonnet or cap. Triangular shape forming a gentle slope over the back of the head when seen in profile.

Fontange　c.1690-1710 a close-fitting linen cap with a tall erection of lace and linen frills in front supported by a wire frame known as the commode. Lappets hang behind.

Forehead cloth　sixteenth and seventeenth centuries, triangular piece of material worn with a coif, the straight edge to the forehead and the point behind. Worn as an extra protection in illness or while sleeping.

Gainsborough　c.1877-80 bonnet or hat with wide curved brim at front only, usually made of dark fabric such as velvet, simply trimmed with ostrich feather.

Head　late seventeenth and eighteenth centuries term usually indicating an indoor cap but sometimes referring to the arrangement of the hair. Shortening for head-dress.

Juliet cap　c.1932-50 skull cap, generally for evening or bridal wear.

Lingerie bonnet or hat　c.1800-1840, and 1895-1910 made of white linen or other washable materials, embroidered or lace trimmed, similar to those used for indoor caps or underwear.

Mushroom crown or hat　eighteenth to twentieth century round crown curving gently inwards towards brim with no join or angle between the two.

Osprey　nineteenth and twentieth centuries, generic term for trimmings made from feathers of rare species of bird of paradise or egret.

Petit bord　1830s-50, evening head-dress usually in form of small hat or toque with narrow brim often in a revived sixteenth century style.

Pillbox　1930s onwards, shallow circular hat with flat crown and no brim made to sit on crown of head exposing most of the hair.

Pinner　late seventeenth century, an indoor cap with lappets. Eighteenth century, a flat circular cap with a frill, worn high on the head.

Poke bonnet　end of eighteenth and nineteenth centuries, bonnet with brim projecting forwards over face.

Poking hat　1799 with a peak projecting forwards like a beak.

Pork pie　1860s a hat with a soft round crown with a stiffened brim turned up close all round.

Postboy　1885-8 hat with a high tapered crown with a flat top, and narrow brim turned up at the back and sides and down at front, forming a point.

Pouch hat　1934 high soft crown of fabric made to fold flat, with narrow band or brim.

Round-eared cap　c.1730-60, small indoor cap worn on top of the head with single or double frill as border to the front only, ending at the ears. With or without lappets.

Spanish hat　1804-12, fabric covered hat of silk or velvet with brim rolled back at the front, and trimmed with ostrich feathers.

Spoon bonnet　1863-5, bonnet with brim rising up at a sharp angle above forehead but curved inwards over cheeks.

Toque　nineteenth and twentieth centuries close-fitting turban hat without a brim, especially popular c.1880-1920s.

Toreador　c.1890s-1905 circular hat with flat top and close turned-up brim forming a broad vertical band.

Tyrolean or Tyrolese hat　late 1860s, felt hat with tapering flat topped crown and brim rolled up at sides.

Yeoman hat　1800-1812 soft crown gathered into a close band or brim.

Hat Collections

Listed below are some of the outstanding museum collections which the author has viewed. Many museums which have no or few hats on display may have a small collection in store which would be worth studying. For a list of museums with costume collections see Janet Arnold's *A Handbook of Costume* (Macmillan).

The Museum of Costume, The Assembly Rooms, Alfred Street, Bath BA1 2QH.
A very fine collection with quite a large number of hats used in the displays. Especially interesting is the collection of twentieth-century hats donated by friends of the founder of the Museum, Mrs Langley Moore, herself a keen hat enthusiast. (A collection of over 150 hats worn by herself from 1925 to 1975 was sold at Christies in March 1980.) The collection at Bath includes hats worn by Margot Fonteyn, Martita Hunt and the Ranee of Pudakota. Some bills and correspondence between the latter and Caroline Reboux in the 1920s are housed at the Costume Research Centre, 4 The Circus, Bath, along with fashion plates and other useful material.

Royal Albert Memorial Museum, Queen Street, Exeter EX4 3RX.
A small collection containing a very high proportion of hats of outstanding quality and condition, especially for the late nineteenth century. Some hats are displayed on models in the Costume Gallery. The collection of twelve eighteenth-century hats formerly on loan there and described in an article in *Costume VII*, 1973, was put up for auction at Sotheby's in March 1981 and is now dispersed, some items being purchased by British museums.

The Museum of London, London Wall, London EC2Y 5HN.
A large and comprehensive collection. Items worn by royalty include three bonnets in excellent condition, worn by Queen Victoria, c.1845-55. The Rose Vernier archive, exhibited at the museum in 1980, includes several hats and a large collection of publicity photos and literature relating to this milliner of Viennese origin who was patronized by royal and society ladies during 1940s-60s. Hats are only occasionally featured in the museum displays, which relate to the history of London.

Victoria and Albert Museum, South Kensington, London SW7 2RL.
This collection is disappointingly small in some respects, but includes the superb Beaton collection. This was exhibited in 1971 and includes examples of highly fashionable hats worn by society women from the 1920s to the 1970s. Some hats worn by Cecil Beaton himself in the late 1960s are also in the collection. A group of men's hats presented by T. W. Christy and Co. includes some genuine early nineteenth-century specimens plus others made at a later date for exhibition purposes. The collection of hats worn by Heather Firbank in the Edwardian period are especially interesting since some of the original bills and shop catalogues are also preserved.

Museum and Art Gallery, Wardown Park, New Bedford Road, Luton LU2 7HA.
A fascinating specialist collection of hats, tools, machinery, sample books, trade catalogues, journals, etc., relating to the straw hat industry in Luton and south-east Midlands from its origins in the late eighteenth century to the present day. A permanent exhibition illustrates methods of straw plaiting and hat manufacture, with examples of straw hats.

The Gallery of English Costume, Platt Hall, Rusholme, Manchester M14 5LL.
A very large collection of consistently high quality, especially good for the nineteenth century. Hats are featured on their own in a small display room and also on models in the period galleries. The museum also includes a library within the store with a good collection of books, magazines and photographs.

Index

94